The Complete Chutney Cookbook:

Add Flavor to Your Life with Spicy Indian Sauces

Rekha Sharma

Ⓥ =VEGAN Ⓟ= QUICK PRESSURE COOKER RECIPE

About the Author _____ *1*

Introduction _____ *1*

Indian Meals _____ *2*

Using this Book _____ *3*

Know Your Measurements _____ 4

Indian Spices and Seasonings _____ *5*

Indian cooking 101 _____ *12*

Basic Techniques _____ 12
Blanching Raw Nuts Ⓥ _____ 13
Almonds (Badaam) _____ 13
Pistachios (Pista) _____ 13
Deep-frying the Indian Way _____ 14
Dry-Roasting Spices, Nuts, and Flours Ⓥ _____ 14
Spices (Masalae) _____ 15
Nuts and Seeds (Maevae) _____ 15
Chickpea and Other Flours (Besan aur Doosrae Aatae) _____ 16
Reconstituting Dried Wild Mushrooms _____ 16
Roasting and Grilling Vegetables Ⓥ _____ 17
Eggplants (Baingan) _____ 17
Bell Peppers (Shimla Mirch) _____ 18
Slivering Blanched Nuts Ⓥ _____ 19
Sprouting Beans and Seeds Ⓥ _____ 20

Basic Ingredients _____ 20
Coconut Milk Ⓥ _____ 20
Crispy Chickpea Batter Drops Ⓥ _____ 21
Crispy Fried Fresh Ginger Ⓥ _____ 22
Crispy Fried Onions Ⓥ _____ 23
Homemade Yogurt _____ 23
Indian Clarified Butter _____ 24
Paneer Cheese _____ 25
Yogurt Cheese _____ 26

Basic Spice Blends _____ 27
Curry Powders _____ 28

 Basic Curry Powder (V) _____ 28
 Spiced Basic Curry Powder (V) _____ 28
 Goan Curry Powder (V) _____ 29
 Gujarati Curry Powder (V) _____ 30
 Kashmiri Curry Powder (V) _____ 31
 Marathi Curry Powder (V) _____ 32
 South Indian Curry Powder (V) _____ 33
Garam Masalas _____ 34
 Basic Garam Masala (V) _____ 34
 Hyderabadi Garam Masala (V) _____ 34
 Kashmiri Garam Masala (V) _____ 35
 Mughlai Garam Masala (V) _____ 36
 Parsi Garam Masala (V) _____ 37
Savory Spice Blends _____ 37
 Chaat Masala (V) _____ 38
 New Delhi Street Food Masala (V) _____ 38
 Bombay Bread-Snack Masala (V) _____ 39
 Cumin-Water Masala (V) _____ 40
 Griddle-Fried Bread Masala (V) _____ 41
 Stuffed Griddle-Fried Bread Masala (V) _____ 41
 Roasted Chile Pepper and Red Peppercorn Masala (V) _____ 42
 Roasted Cumin and Fenugreek Masala (V) _____ 43
 Roasted Cumin-Pepper Masala (V) _____ 44
 Punjabi Raita and Buttermilk Masala (V) _____ 44
 Kashmiri Raita Masala (V) _____ 45
Masala Blends for Special Dishes _____ 46
 Bengali Five Whole Spice Blend (V) _____ 46
 Braised Meat Masala (V) _____ 46
 Chickpea Masala (V) _____ 47
 Grilling Masala (V) _____ 48
 Gujrati Masala (V) _____ 49
 Meat Masala (V) _____ 50
 Vindaloo Masala (V) _____ 51
 Wok Masala (V) _____ 52
Special South Indian Blends _____ 52
 Sambar Masala (V) _____ 53
 Rasam Masala (V) _____ 53
 Chutney Coconut Masala (V) _____ 54
 Lentil Paste (V) _____ 55
 Peanut Masala (V) _____ 56

    Sesame Masala Ⓥ 57

    Thenga Masala Ⓥ 57

  Dessert and Tea Masalas 58

    Dessert Masala Ⓥ 58

    Tea Masala Ⓥ 59

BASIC FLAVORING PASTES 60

  Basic Ginger Paste Ⓥ 60

  Basic Garlic Paste Ⓥ 60

  Roasted Garlic Paste Ⓥ 61

  Basic Ginger-Garlic Paste Ⓥ 62

  Almond and Poppy Seed Paste Ⓥ 62

  Basic Cashew Paste Ⓥ 63

  Basic Curry Paste with Onion Ⓥ 63

  Basic Curry Paste without Onion 64

  Basic Ginger and Green Chile Pepper Paste Ⓥ 65

  Basic Onion Paste Ⓥ 65

  Boiled Onion Paste Ⓥ 66

  Chile Pepper Paste Ⓥ 67

  Fried Onion Paste 67

  Goan Vindaloo Paste Ⓥ 68

  Gujarati Green Paste Ⓥ 69

  Hyderabadi Ginger-Garlic Paste Ⓥ 69

  Kerala Fried Onion Paste Ⓥ 70

  Minty Green Curry Paste Ⓥ 71

  Mughlai Curry Paste with Nuts 71

  Spicy Yellow Curry Paste Ⓥ 72

  Tamarind Paste Ⓥ 73

Chutney 74

Green Chutneys 74

  Basic Green Chutney Ⓥ 74

  Cilantro-Lime Chutney Ⓥ 75

  Mint Chutney Ⓥ 76

  Mint-Garlic Chutney Ⓥ 77

  Scallion-Ginger Chutney 78

  South Indian Cilantro Chutney Ⓥ 79

Coconut Chutneys 79

  Fresh Coconut Chutney with Cilantro 80

  Minty Coconut-Tamarind Chutney Ⓥ 81

Roasted Coconut Chutney Ⓥ	82
Semolina-Coconut Chutney	83
Shredded Coconut Chutney Ⓥ	84

Garlic and Chile Pepper Chutneys — 84

Garlic and Fresh Red Chile Pepper Chutney Ⓥ	85
Green Garlic and Nuts Chutney Ⓥ	86
Peanut and Garlic Chutney Ⓥ	87

Bean and Legume Chutneys — 88

Classic Hyderabadi Ginger-Sesame Chutney Ⓥ	88
Roasted Black Chickpea Chutney with Peanuts Ⓥ	89
Roasted Dal and Fresh Green Chile Pepper Chutney Ⓥ	90
Sesame-Peanut Chutney Ⓥ	90

Yogurt Chutneys — 91

Yogurt Cheese Chutney with Minced Greens	91
Yogurt Chutney with Puréed Greens	92
Yogurt Chutney with Roasted Dals and Spices	93
Yogurt-Almond Chutney	94

Puréed Fruit Chutneys — 95

Puréed Fresh Mango-Ginger Chutney Ⓥ	95
Puréed Green Mango Chutney Ⓥ	96
South Indian Tomato Chutney Ⓥ	97
Tart Apple-Ginger Chutney Ⓥ	98

Preserved Chutneys — 99

Cranberry Chutney Preserve Ⓥ	99
Fragrant Mango Chutney Preserve Ⓥ	100
Red Tomato Chutney Preserve Ⓥ	101
Spicy Apple-Ginger Chutney Preserve Ⓥ	102
Spicy Apricot Chutney Preserve Ⓥ	103
Tomato Chutney Preserve Ⓥ	104

Sonth Chutneys — 105

Minty Sonth Chutney with Mango Ⓥ	106
Sonth Chutney with Dried Mango Slices Ⓥ Ⓟ	107
Sonth Chutney with Fresh and Dried Fruits Ⓥ	108
Sweet Sonth Chutney with Dates Ⓥ	109

Endnote — *110*

ABOUT THE AUTHOR

Rekha Sharma was born in "Jalandhar", a small city in the Indian state of "Punjab". Her father was in the Indian army, because of which her family used to move around a lot. By a very young age, Rekha had experienced cuisines from all over India, and every time she travelled to a new area and tried new local cuisines, her passion and fascination for Indian food grew. She completed M. Phil. in English from a reputed Indian University, and then became a college professor for a few years. She got married at a young age of 23, and left her job as a college professor when she had her first child. By the age of 26, she was a mother of two- a son and a daughter, and was mostly house-bound. As she started cooking for four, her passion for cooking reignited, and she started giving cooking classes on the side. She worked as a part time cook until her kids became independent, and then she opened her own restaurant in Delhi, India. Today, she is 50+ years old, manages a restaurant, and writes Indian cookbooks on the side. She is best known for "A Taste of India", a series of Indian cookbooks.

INTRODUCTION

India is a huge landmass which contains mountains, deserts, plateaus, plains, beaches, and islands. Politically, it is divided into 28 states, and most of these states have their own languages and cultures. Even within a political state you will find multiple small villages with their own sub-languages and cultures. Needless to say, India is a land of variety, and this variety shows in its cuisine. Indian restaurants are everywhere, and if you've been through the menu of one, you know what I'm talking about.

North India is a land of flatbreads, while South India is a land of rice. India has a coastline that stretches for 7,516.6 km (4,671 miles), and you can find a wide variety of seafood here, depending on which part of the coastline you're at. Not just the ingredients, but the preparation methods also differ from region to region. If you're in the eastern state of West Bengal, you will see them prepare fish with mustard and turmeric. On the other hand, if you're in Kerala, you will watch them use coconut instead.

Majority of the people in India are Hindus, and the truly devout Hindus are usually vegetarian. Vegetarianism is especially prevalent in central India. The primary source of protein in these vegetarian dominated areas is- beans, grains, lentils, peas, etc. Indians usually refer to these as "Dal". Indian food has less meat and more vegetables, which make Indian food great for health, and also for the environment. The cooking methods used in this book make the recipes as healthy as possible without compromising the authentic Indian taste. You will find that the majority of recipes in this book are Vegan, and you can identify a vegan recipe from the "Ⓥ" symbol. Also, in India, the pressure cooker is highly popular, and hence you will find quite a few pressure cooker recipes in this book. Recipes cooked in a pressure cooker are generally very quick to make, and in this book, you can identify those recipes from the symbol "Ⓟ".

In this book, you will find delicious recipes from all over India. Most of the recipes in this book are simple, and if you're a "newbie" when it comes to cooking, this book will serve you well. You will, however, need to learn to source some of the ingredients that aren't commonly used in American cooking. If you can't find an ingredient in a local store, you can always find it on amazon.com. If there is a local Indian or ethnic market close to your home, you're in luck! Also, a pressure cooker is an indispensable tool to have in your kitchen, so invest in one if you haven't already.

INDIAN MEALS

Typically, an Indian meal contains a wet or dry dish of meat or vegetables, or both. This dish is typically eaten with an Indian flatbread, or rice. If the food is spicy, which it usually is, there is plain yogurt on the side to soothe the flavour, and also to aid with digestion. If one wishes to add a little more punch to the meal, he/she can have a pickle or chutney on the side. Salads are also quite common side dishes.

If cooking for guests, we Indians usually go for slightly "fancier" versions of the staples. Plain yogurt may be replaced by "raita" (plain yogurt with added spices and other ingredients), plain rice may be replaced by fried or seasoned rice dishes, and fried flatbreads called "paranthas" may be used. We usually offer starters and desserts to guests too.

For everyday eating, however, I will advise you to stick to the healthier low-calorie stuff. Vegetables are a staple in the Indian diet, and for good reason. A balanced meal has a good balance of carbohydrates, fiber, protein, and fat. The diet should be rich in other vitamins and minerals too, which Indian food usually is, thanks to the presence of vegetables, legumes, and grains.

Another thing you need to consider is how much spice you like. It is possible to add more later, but impossible to extract the spice once added, so it is usually a good idea to add the spice incrementally, tasting the food as you add. You will only need to do this once or twice though. Once you know what you like, and how much you can handle, go all out!

USING THIS BOOK

In this book, I will call for cooking appliances that are readily available in almost every kitchen. I understand that it is not possible to have a "tandoor" (a large cylindrical clay or metal oven used in traditional Indian cooking and baking) in your kitchen. The tandoor can be replicated by what is readily available in your kitchen, and I will clearly detail in the directions of each recipe what you need to do.

In order to prepare the recipes in this book, you will need a stove, an oven, a pressure cooker, and a microwave in a few cases. A food processor will also come in handy as it will save you a lot of hassle.

It is usually a good idea to prepare things like spice pastes, chutneys, spice powders, and other perishable basic ingredients in bulk, and in advance. These ingredients are best stored in the freezer, so if you have one, make sure you use it. Here are a few basic tips and tricks to know before you dive into the recipes:

- Read the full list of ingredients and directions before you commit to a recipe. Make sure you have all the ingredients and all the appliances used in the directions. You can make almost every spice blend used in this book easily at home, but you can also buy these at a store. I'll leave the decision to you. You can find almost anything online these days.
- A lot of the recipes in this book will call for ingredients like cilantro, dry-roasted cumin, sesame seeds, black peppercorns, ginger paste, garlic paste, ginger-garlic paste, green chutney, crispy fried ginger, crispy fried onions; fresh lemon juice; paneer (Cottage cheese), mango and lemon pickles, and some chutneys. If you

- want to add Indian recipes to your arsenal, and wish to prepare these regularly, you will do well to make these ingredients a staple in your pantry.
- Start the cooking process when you're good and ready, and have everything you need ready, and in front of you.
- It is always a good idea to add a little less salt and seasoning if you're not sure how much you will need. Taste your food as you go to hit that perfect spot. If, however, you do add more than you can handle by mistake, you have a few options. Throw in a peeled and chopped potato, or try eating the dish with yogurt on the side. You can also make some more of the dish, this time without the spice, and then add it to the over-spiced batch.

KNOW YOUR MEASUREMENTS

American cooks use standard containers, the 8-ounce cup and a tablespoon that takes exactly 16 level fillings to fill that cup level. Measuring by cup makes it very difficult to give weight equivalents, as the density plays an important role when it comes to weight. The easiest way therefore to deal with cup measurements in recipes is to take the amount by volume rather than by weight. Thus, the equation reads:

1 cup = 240ml = 8 fluid Ounces

½ cup = 120ml = 4 fluid ounces

It is possible to buy a set of American cup measures in major stores around the world.

In the States, butter is sometimes measured in sticks. One stick is the equivalent of 8 tablespoons. One tablespoon of butter is therefore the equivalent to ½ ounce/15 grams.

Liquid Measures

1 Teaspoon= 5 Millilitres

1 Tablespoon = 14 millilitres

2 Tablespoons= 1 Fluid Ounce

Solid Measures

1 Ounce= 28 Grams

16 Ounces= 1 Pound

INDIAN SPICES AND SEASONINGS

"Spicy" is the first thing that comes to mind when we think of Indian food, and for good reason. Historically, Indian spices have been one of India's greatest exported commodities. Indian spices go best with all kinds of food! Go out there and play around! In this section, we will look at a few of the most popular spices. If you cannot find a particular spice in a nearby store, you will surely find it online on amazon.com.

AJWAIN SEEDS

Ajwain, ajowan, or Trachyspermum ammi—also known as ajowan caraway, bishop's weed, or carom—is an annual herb in the family Apiaceae. Both the leaves and the seed-like fruit of the plant are fit for consumption. The name "bishop's weed" also is a common name for other plants. These tiny brown or green-brown, ridged, celery seed look-alikes seem fragrance-free at first, but when crushed, they emit an intense and highly aromatic, thyme-like aroma, which calms down once cooked. When eaten raw, they have an intensely fiery and pungent bite. *Ajwain* seeds are an amazing home remedy to relieve gas and stomachaches, and are frequently chewed raw by people with seasoned tastes.

ASAFOETIDA

Called *Hing* or *heeng* in Hindi, Asafoetida is a plant that has a bad pungent smell and tastes bitter. It is sometimes even referred to as "devil's dung." People use asafoetida resin, a gum-like material, as medicine. Asafoetida resin is produced by solidifying juice that comes out of cuts made in the plant's living roots. When cooked, however, it adds a pleasant onion-garlic flavour to the food. It also has numerous health benefits such as- it relieves flatulence, enhances digestion, acts as an antibiotic, etc. It is an indispensable part of Indian cuisine. Ground Asafoetida is used in recipes. It is usually a good idea to buy lumps or granules, and grind it before using in a recipe. Buy your asafoetida in lumps (or fine granules) and then grind them at home. If you wish to buy the already ground version from the market, remember that it might not be 100% pure.

BAY LEAVES

Called *Tejpatta, tejpat,* or *tej patra* in Hindi, the bay leaf is an aromatic leaf commonly used in cooking. It can be used whole, or as dried and ground. There are two varieties commonly available: the leaves of the bay laurel found typically in the Western world, and those of the Indian cassia tree. Both work fine, but if you can get your hands on the Indian version, it will make the recipes slightly more "Indian". Doesn't matter much, though.

BLACK SALT

Called *Kaala namak* in Hindi, black salt is a kiln-fired rock salt commonly used in South Asian regions. It has a sulphurous, pungent-smell. It is also known as "Himalayan black salt", Sulemani namak, bit lobon, kala noon, or pada loon and manufactured from the salts mined in the regions surrounding the Himalayas.

CARDAMOM PODS

Called *Elaichi* in Hindi, Cardamom (or cardamom) is a spice made from the seeds of several plants in the genera Elettaria and Amomum in the family Zingiberaceae. Both genera are native to the Indian subcontinent and Indonesia. Two variety of this are commonly available: small green ones (called hari or chhoti elaichi in Hindi), and large black ones (Called badi or kaali elaichi in Hindi). The green ones have a strong refreshing fragrance, while the big black ones have a milder woody-smoky aroma. Both are great home remedies to treat and manage gas, and also for nausea and vomiting. They also work as a healthy natural mouth freshener.

CHILES, FRESH GREEN AND DRIED RED

Called *Mirch* or *mirchi* in Hindi, chile peppers—fresh green (*hari mirch*) and dried red (*laal mirch*)—are members of the capsicum family. Green chiles are usually young, and they turn red as they age. The younger greener chilies have a much stronger hotter flavour compared to the red ones. The red chiles are dried and ground into a red powder, which is a staple ingredient in Indian dishes. If you're living in a different part of the world, look for "cayenne powder" in a nearby store or online if you cannot find pure red chile powder. Chiles are great for health too, and enhance digestion. They are used in powerful sinus, cough, and cold home remedies. Just ensure you don't touch any sensitive areas of your body if you've just handled it.

CINNAMON AND CASSIA

Called *Dalchini* or *darchini* in Hindi, Cinnamon is a common ingredient in kitchens all around the world, and is commonly available in ground, or stick form. Cinnamon adds a pleasant fragrance to foods, and is great for the digestive system.

CLOVES

Called *Laung* or *lavang* in Hindi, Cloves are the aromatic flower buds of a tree in the family Myrtaceae, Syzygium aromaticum. They have a strong aroma, and a strong sweet and sour taste. They are great for digestion, and relieving gas.

CORIANDER SEEDS AND GREENS

Called *Dhania, sookha*, and *patta* or *hara* in Hindi, Coriander is an annual herb in the family Apiaceae. It is also known as Chinese parsley, and in the United States the stems and leaves are commonly referred to as cilantro. The whole of the plant is fit for consumption, but fresh leaves and dried seeds are most commonly used in cooking. The fresh green leaves have a sweet citrus flavour, and smell absolutely fantastic. These are highly perishable so use them as soon as possible, and always store them in your fridge.

CUMIN AND BLACK CUMIN

Called *Jeera* or *zeera* in Hindi, Cumin is a flowering plant in the family Apiaceae, native to southwestern Asia including the Middle East. Its seeds – each one contained within a fruit, which is dried – are a staple in the Indian kitchen. They have a strong spicy aroma, and a bitter taste. It is great for the stomach.

CURRY LEAVES

Called *Meethineem* or *karipatta* in Hindi, Curry leaves from from the curry leaf tree, which is a tropical to sub-tropical tree in the family Rutaceae, and is native to India. Curry leaves are a staple in Indian cooking, and quite a few recipes in this book will call for this ingredient. They taste slightly bitter, but taste absolutely amazing in certain recipes.

FENNEL SEEDS

Called *Saunf* in Hindi, Fennel seeds come from Fennel, which is a flowering plant species in the carrot family. They appear long, ridged, oval or curved, and green-yellow in color. They have an aromatic pleasant taste, and are great for the digestive system.

FENUGREEK SEEDS AND GREENS

Called *Daana-methi* or *metharae* and *patta* or *hari methi* in Hindi, Fenugreek seeds are the dried, angular, yellow-brown seeds of a highly aromatic annual herb of the legume family. They are widely grown in India, and taste bitter when eaten raw. Luckily, they aren't meant to be eaten raw. When stir-fried or dry-roasted, these turn into something quite delicious.

GINGER

Called *Adrak, taaza,* and *sookha* in Hindi, Ginger needs no introduction. This juicy underground stem has a strong taste and is great for health. When buying ginger, ensure you get the fresh juicy ones. If you see any signs of dryness, shriveling, or mold, you should probably not pick that particular one.

KALONJI

You might know of these as—nigella, onion seeds, black onion seeds, black caraway seeds, or black cumin seeds. In Hindi, however, it is called *kalonji*, and that is the term commonly used outside India too, so that is what I will call it in this book. These little charcoal black triangular seeds look a lot like onion seeds. They have a light flavour like oregano, and taste bitter when raw. After cooking, however, these start to emit a nutty aroma and taste.

KOKUM

Also known as *cocum, cocamful,* and fish tamarind, *Kokum* is the sun-dried rind of a ½- to 1-inch fruit of the mangosteen-oil tree. The ripe fruits are eaten too, but the majority of them is dried into rather sticky, sour, purple-black pieces of *kokum*, a delicious spice. If a recipe calls for this ingredient, and you can't find it, Tamarind can be used instead.

MANGO POWDER

Called *Amchur* in Hindi, Mango powder is a fruity spice powder made from dried unripe green mangoes and is used as a citrusy seasoning in Indian cuisine. It is mostly produced in India, and is used as a citrus seasoning, and also to Put in the nutritional benefits of mangoes when the fresh fruit is out of season.

MINT

Called *Pudina*, *taaza*, and *sookha* in Hindi, Mint needs no introduction as it is one of the most popular herbs in the entire world. These are a staple in the Indian kitchen too, and when buying mint, ensure you get fresh aromatic leaves.

MIXED MELON SEEDS

Called *Char-magaz* in Hindi, this is basically a mixture of seeds from four different summer melons—cantaloupe, watermelon, cucumber, and pumpkin. The seeds are free of fragrance, and have a very mild taste similar to pumpkin. These are loaded with zinc, iron, and potassium, and are great for the brain.

MUSTARD SEEDS AND GREENS

Called *Raayi* or *rai*, and *sarson* in Hindi, Mustard is popular all over the world. The most common use of mustard seeds we see today is to make mustard oil, which is a healthy and cheap cooking oil which is a staple in kitchens all over the world. These are loaded with Vitamins A and C, Iron, and Calcium, making them a prominent health food. They have a very strong taste by themselves, but go well in quite a few Indian dishes, as you will see soon enough.

NUTMEG AND MACE

Called *Jaiphul* and *javitri* in Hindi, Nutmeg and mace are two different varieties of spices obtained from the same apricot-like fruit of a tall evergreen tree. Nutmeg is a wrinkly, medium brown, 1-inch oval nut that resides inside the thin, brittle, shiny outer shell of a ripe nutmeg seed. To obtain nutmeg, the shell has to be broken.

Mace is the lacy, web-like coating around the outside of the nutmeg shell. This dazzling coating is cautiously removed after the fruit is broken open, and is then flattened and dried to become brittle yellow-orange mace, ready to use.

They are both great for health, and vital ingredients for the pharmaceutical industry.

PAPRIKA

Called *Kashmiri degi mirch* or *rang vaali mirch* in Hindi, Indian paprika is the vivid red powder made from mild, non-pungent red chiles. Although made from red chiles, it does not taste very hot, and is primarily used for its color. It is an indispensable part of the Indian pantry.

BLACK PEPPER

Called *Kaalimirch* in Hindi, Black pepper is often called the king of all spices. It is one of the oldest and most popular spices on this planet. Naturally, it is a staple in the Indian kitchen, and can be sprinkled over pretty much any recipe in this book.

DRIED POMEGRANATE SEEDS

Called *Anaardana* in Hindi, dried pomegranate seeds are basically sun-dried or dehydrated fruity seeds and the flesh of a wild pomegranate tree. They have a sweet and fruity fragrance, and are a common ingredient in Indian cooking.

POPPY SEEDS

Called *Khas-khas* in Hindi, poppy seeds are oilseeds obtained from opium poppy. Poppy seeds come in many colors, but the Indian versions are pale yellow. If a recipe calls for poppy seeds, feel free to use any kind of poppy seeds you wish.

ROSE WATER AND ESSENCE

Called *Gulaab jal* and *ruh gulaab* in Hindi, rose water and rose essence are made from the petals of specially cultivated highly fragrant red roses. Rose water is basically water with a strong fragrance of roses. Small bottles of rose water are easily available in stores.

SAFFRON

Called *Kaesar* or *zaffron* in Hindi, Saffron is one of the priciest spices available out there, and hence should be used sparingly if you're on a budget. Almost all of Indian saffron comes from Kashmir in North India. It has an exotic flavour and imparts a yellow color to the dishes it is used in.

SCREWPINE ESSENCE

Called *Kewda* or *ruh kewra* in Hindi, screwpine is the essence made from the flowers of a tropical tree with narrow, sword-like leaves. Think of this as rose water with a different fragrance.

SESAME SEEDS AND OIL

Called *Til* or *gingelly* in Hindi, sesame seeds are the tiny, smooth, oval, flat seeds of an annual tropical herb. When raw, these have almost no aroma, but when dry-roasted, these develop a nutty flavour.

SILVER LEAVES

Called *Chandi ka verk* or *vark* in Hindi, silver leaves are primarily used as a garnish, and don't really add anything to the flavour. This is used in Indian recipes to make them look exotic.

STAR ANISE

Called *Badian, badiyan, dodhful, dodphul*, and *anasphal* in Hindi, star anise is the dried mahogany-colored, 8-pointed, star-shaped fruit of a big evergreen tree. It has a sweet flavour, and is an ingredient in quite a few Indian recipes.

TAMARIND

Called *Imli* in Hindi, tamarind has a highly sour taste, and is a staple in the Indian kitchen. It is rich in vitamin C, and good for digestion, fighting throat infections, and fighting mild colds.

TURMERIC

Called *Haldi* in Hindi, turmeric is a common ingredient in Indian curries. It has a warm and bitter taste, and one of the healthiest spices out there. It is a natural antiseptic, an anti-inflammatory agent, and a blood purifier. Turmeric is used in quite a few home remedies such as soothing aches and pains.

INDIAN COOKING 101

If you've never cooked a single Indian recipe in your life, this section is for you. Learn your basics, follow my guidance, and practice till you make it. Do I make it sound hard? Do I make it sound like a chore? I don't know, but Indian cooking is none of those things. Indian cooking is actually quite easy, once you get the hang of it.

There are a few basic techniques used in Indian cooking that you might need to learn if you're new to cooking. Luckily, you don't really need to do these things by yourself as you can easily find dry-roasted ingredients and pre-mixed spice blends in the market. If, however, you wish to make these on your own, I will teach you to do so, just in case you wish to have a little more control over your ingredients in the future. Oh, and I personally enjoy doing these things a lot, so try it out, maybe dry roasting will become your new hobby!

Most of the basic gadgets and appliances this book will call for are quite common even in the American kitchen. I will still list these basic tools below. Feel free to improvise if you don't have one of these, and don't wish to invest in one yet.

- Concave cast-iron tava griddle to make breads
- Non-stick or cast-iron
- Round-bottomed wok (called kadhai in India)
- Pressure Cooker
- Food processor

If you can't find these in a store nearby, they are easily available on amazon.com.

In this book, you can identify a vegan and a pressure cooker recipe simply by looking for the following symbols by their names:

- Ⓥ= **Vegan**
- Ⓟ= **Quick Pressure Cooker Recipe**

BASIC TECHNIQUES

In this section we will learn a few basic techniques you will need to do the most authentic Indian cooking.

BLANCHING RAW NUTS

This technique is called "Bhigona aur chheelna" in Hindi

Basically this technique is all about immersing the ingredients in water until their skins become soft, and then peeling them off. You can buy pre-blanched stuff in the market, but where's the fun in that? Where's the freshness? And most importantly, where's that Indian feel?

Yield: ½ cup

ALMONDS (BADAAM)

There are two ways of blanching almonds.

Traditional Method

1. Immerse ½ cup shelled raw almonds 8 to 24 hours in sufficient water to cover by minimum two inches. (This allows the nuts to absorb the water and soften.)
2. Drain and peel the skin off each one using your fingers.

Quick Method

1. Immerse and boil ½ cup almonds in water until the skins absorb the water and become loose, approximately five minutes.
2. Allow to cool, then peel.

PISTACHIOS (PISTA)

Removing the outer skin of pistachios is much easier compared to almonds.

1. Put ½ cup shelled, raw pistachios in a small stainless steel (not nonstick) saucepan, with sufficient water to cover by minimum one inch, and bring to a boil using high heat.

2. Turn off the heat and set aside to soften, approximately one hour. Drain and put them on a sanitized kitchen towel. Cover using a different towel (or fold the first one over) and rub on the towel using your hands. As you do this, the loosened skin will get removed.

DEEP-FRYING THE INDIAN WAY

This recipe is called "Talna" in Hindi

Yield: 20 to 30 pieces

Indian deep-frying is basic as it gets. You take a Chinese wok (or a "kadhaai" as we call in Hindi) and you pour in a good amount of oil, sufficient to completely submerge the ingredients you need to fry, you then heat the oil and throw the ingredients into the heated oil.

Ingredients:

- 1½ to 2 cups oil
- 20 to 30 pieces of food

Directions:

1. Heat the oil using moderate to high heat until it achieves 325°F to 350°F on a frying thermometer. At this temperature, if you throw in a small piece of food, it will take about fifteen to twenty seconds to come to the surface of the oil. This temperature is important, as too high or too low can lead to less than ideal results.
2. Put food pieces into the wok, without overcrowding. Fry until a golden colour is achieved, approximately one minute. Using a slotted spatula, hold each piece against the edge of the wok for a few seconds, to let surplus oil to drain back into the wok. After that, move to a tray coated using paper towels.

DRY-ROASTING SPICES, NUTS, AND FLOURS Ⓥ

This technique is called "Sookha bhunna" in Hindi

Yield: Approximately ½ cup

Basically, we dry-roast dry spices, herbs, nuts, dals (legumes), and selected flours by throwing them into a skillet and browning them in absence of any cooking fat or liquid. This process filters out the unwanted raw flavour, and enhances the flavour of the essential oils, which is what we actually need. Below we will look at a few specific ingredients that we need to dry-roast in Indian cooking.

SPICES (MASALAE)

Pretty much every spice there is can be dry roasted, and a few of the most commonly dry-roasted spices are black peppercorns, coriander, mustard seeds, sesame, cumin, etc.

1. Put ½ cup of any one type of whole seeds in a small sized cast-iron skillet, saucepan, or "tava" and roast using moderate heat, stirring and swaying the pan, until smoke with a strong fragrance starts to rise and the seeds appear slightly darker, approximately two minutes.
2. Turn off the heat and allow to cool down. Using a rolling pin, the back of a big sized spoon, or using a mortar and pestle, squash them until crudely ground. Or, grind them thoroughly using a spice or coffee grinder.
3. Put inside an airtight vessel and place the vessel in a cool, dark place. Can be stored safely for approximately one month at room temperature, or six months in a fridge. Roasted black peppercorns can be ground fresh before every use if you have a pepper mill.

NUTS AND SEEDS (MAEVAE)

1. Beginning with ½ cup whole, chopped, or slivered nuts, put them in a small sized cast-iron skillet, saucepan, or "tava" and roast using moderate heat, stirring and swaying the pan, until a golden colour is achieved (don't let it get brown), approximately two minutes.
2. Turn off the heat and allow to cool down.
3. Use instantly or put inside an airtight vessel and place the vessel in a cool, dark place, approximately seven days at room temperature or approximately thirty days in a fridge.

Tip: Different ingredients roast in different amounts of time, and hence it is a good idea to roast different ingredients individually.

CHICKPEA AND OTHER FLOURS (BESAN AUR DOOSRAE AATAE)

1. Sieve ½ cup flour and put it in a non-stick skillet or saucepan.
2. Roast using moderate to low heat until it starts to look golden and releases its fragrance, approximately three minutes. Stir continuously and shake the pan regularly to avoid lumping and burning.
3. Allow to cool, then put inside an airtight vessel and place the vessel in a cool, dark place, approximately seven days at room temperature or approximately thirty days in a fridge.

RECONSTITUTING DRIED WILD MUSHROOMS

This technique is called "Sookhi khumbon ko bhigona" in Hindi

Yield: 1 cup reconstituted mushrooms

Mushrooms are commonly available in dried form. So, you will need to rehydrate them before using in a recipe. Here's how.

Ingredients:

- 1 ounce dried wild mushrooms

Directions:

1. Rinse the mushrooms, then immerse in water to cover by minimum two inches until they absorb the water and bloat up, approximately one hour. Rinse them again under running water to eliminate all dirt that may still be sticking to them. Chop and use as required.

2. Strain the mushroom-soaking water through a coffee filter or paper towels until it seems thoroughly clean and dirt free. Use it in soups, rice pullaos (pilafs), and curries.

ROASTING AND GRILLING VEGETABLES

This technique is called "Sabziyan bhunna" in Hindi

Roasting and grilling vegetables is the first step in preparing quite a few Indian recipes, and you will need to know how it is done before you dive into the recipes. Below, we will look at how to roast a few of the most commonly roasted ingredients.

EGGPLANTS (BAINGAN)

Yield: Approximately 1½ cups of pulp from each pound of eggplant

When buying eggplants, ensure you grab the young ones. You can identify these by their weight. Young eggplants usually weigh less for their size, and have a silky smooth skin with no signs of deterioration. Also, smaller eggplants are much easier to cook than the bigger ones, for obvious reasons.

The easiest and most convenient way to roast eggplants today is to just place them directly over your gas burners. If you don't want to make a mess of your stove, use a grill too. The best way, however, is to use coals and a grill, just like the Indians have done it for centuries.

Directions to Fire-Roast Eggplants:

1. Rinse, dry, and cover your hands with a thin layer of oil, and rub them over the surface of each eggplant. Next, use a sharp kitchen knife to pierce the skin in a few places. Put over scorching coals of a grill if possible, or over the direct flame of a kitchen stove burner(coat the lowermost plate using aluminium foil), and roast, rotating using kitchen tonga as the sides turn black, until the eggplant is very soft and the skin is thoroughly charred, approximately five to seven minutes. Move to a container and allow to cool down.

2. Once cool sufficient to hold, peel off and discard the charred skin. You will have to wash your fingers multiple times as you do this. Do not rinse the eggplants. Mash the pulp using your hands or a fork until fairly smooth but still lumpy. Do not make a fully smooth purée; a little texture is required. Strain and stir in any juices that may have collected in the container. Store in the fridge for approximately five days or approximately four months in the freezer.

Directions to Oven-Roast Eggplants:

1. Slightly oil and pierce the skin in a few places using the tip of a knife and bake using an oven pre-heated to 400°F until the eggplants become soft, approximately thirty to forty minutes. You can wrap them using an aluminium foil prior to baking.

Directions to Broil Eggplants:

1. Cut into half along the length and place, skin side up, on a baking tray coated using aluminium foil.
2. Broil 8 to 10 inches from the heat source until the eggplants become soft and the skin seems charred.

BELL PEPPERS (SHIMLA MIRCH)

Yield: Approximately ⅔ cup of pulp from each pound of pepper

Bell peppers are a common ingredient in the Indian kitchen, and taste absolutely amazing when roasted.

Directions to Fire-Roast Bell Peppers:

1. Put whole bell peppers, if possible over the scorching coals of a grill or over the direct flame of the kitchen stove (coat the lowermost plate using aluminium foil) and roast, rotating using kitchen tonga as the sides turn black, until the skin is mildly charred, approximately two to three minutes. (There is no need to oil the bell peppers or poke any holes in them, or to char them completely.)
2. Move to a container, cover or seal using an air-tight bag, and allow to sit for approximately fifteen minutes. This enables the peppers to sweat and cool down, making them simple to peel. Peel the peppers, eliminating as much of the burned skin as possible. You may leave some mildly charred skin on for flavour.

Do not rinse them using water. Rinse your hands as required. Eliminate the stems and seeds and chop or purée the peppers; if any juice has accumulated in the container, strain it and add it to the purée.

Directions to Oven-Roast Bell Peppers:

1. Rinse, dry, and cut each bell pepper into halves or quarters, lengthwise. Put on a baking sheet, with the cut side down. Put the sheet on the center rack of the oven, start the broiler, and roast until charred, approximately eight to ten minutes. Flip over once.
2. Put ¼ cup water on the baking sheet to dissolve most of the browned juice and use it in soups, rice, breads, or vegetables.

To Broil Bell Peppers

1. Rinse, dry, and seed the bell peppers, then cut them into 1-inch or larger pieces.
2. Put on a baking sheet coated using aluminium foil.
3. Broil 4 to 5 inches from the heat source, flipping over once or twice until the pieces are mildly charred.

SLIVERING BLANCHED NUTS

This technique is called "Mavae kaatna" in Hindi

Yield: ½ cup

You can buy slivered blanched nuts from the market, but these are done using machines. If you have some free time on your hands, then use your hands. This is a great exercise for improving your hand-eye coordination, and you will get much better and thinner shreds as compared to the mechanical versions.

1. Begin with 1 cup blanched almonds, pistachio, or other nuts.
2. Grab a paring knife in your dominant hand, and hold each nut, one at a time, between the thumb and forefinger of your other hand.
3. Scrape softly lengthwise using a sharp paring knife in tiny top-to-bottom movements.
4. As you do this, frail slivers or shavings will fall from the nut.

SPROUTING BEANS AND SEEDS

This technique is called "Sookhi dalonko phutana" in Hindi

Yield: Approximately 4 cups

Sprouted beans are one of the healthiest ingredients on the planet. Here's how to sprout beans the Indian way.

Ingredients:

- 1 cup any variety whole beans and seeds, picked over and washed
- 1 thick kitchen towel

Directions:

1. Immerse the beans overnight, in water to cover by minimum two inches.
2. Drain thoroughly, cover the container using a lid, then cover using a thick kitchen towel and put in a warm spot in the kitchen like a closet.
3. Check at least once per day and stir them a little if you wish to. Keep the beans mildly moist at all times. If the inside surface of the lid has tiny droplets of water on it, the moisture is right, and the beans should sprout in two to three days.

BASIC INGREDIENTS

Before we start with the recipes, you need to acquaint yourself with a few of the most common ingredients in Indian cooking what you might not have used before.

COCONUT MILK

This recipe is called "Nariyal doodh" in Hindi

Yield: 1 cup thick coconut milk

Coconut milk is different from coconut water. You can buy this in a store, or make your own. Here's how:

Ingredients:

- 1 cup hot water
- 1½ cups grated fresh coconut meat

Directions:

1. Using a food processor or a blender, combine and pulse the coconut and ½ cup of the water until thoroughly smooth. Allow the processed coconut to soak in this water for approximately half an hour. Next, pass the whole thing through the fine mesh of a food mill or a strainer.
2. Put the leftover coconut back into your food processor. Put in the rest of the ½ cup water, then process and strain once more. Combine with the first coconut milk. Add water till your desired consistency is achieved. Use instantly, or store in the fridge for approximately 4 days or freeze for no more than sixty days.

CRISPY CHICKPEA BATTER DROPS

This recipe is called "Boondi" in Hindi

Yield: Approximately 1½ cups

You can buy these ready-made from Indian stores, but you can also make your own. These go great with yogurt!

Ingredients:

- ¼ teaspoon salt, or to taste
- ½ cup water, or as required
- ⅔ cup chickpea flour, sifted
- 1 cup peanut oil for deep frying
- A scant pinch baking soda

Directions:

1. In a container, combine the chickpea flour, salt and baking soda. Put in the water and whisk to make a smooth and creamy batter. Let sit for about ten minutes then whisk once more.
2. Take a small wok, or saucepan, or kadhaai, pour oil into it and heat using moderate to high heat until it achieves 325°F to 350°F on a frying thermometer or until a drop of the batter surges to the surface of the oil almost instantly. Hold a round spatula with holes over the oil and progressively pour the batter through the holes, while shaking and tapping the spatula to ensure the batter falls as drops into the hot oil. Stop pouring when the wok appears to have sufficient drops.
3. Fry one batch until a golden colour is achieved, approximately forty to fifty seconds, then move the drops with another slotted spatula to a tray coated using paper towels, before you start the next batch. Keep doing it till all the batter has been used. Allow to cool, then store in an airtight vessel in the fridge for approximately three months or in the freezer about six months.

CRISPY FRIED FRESH GINGER

This recipe is called "Bhuna adrak" in Hindi

Yield: Approximately 1 cup

Ginger is a great garnish and a flavour booster!

Ingredients:

- ½ pound fresh ginger, peeled and cut into thin matchsticks
- ½ teaspoon salt, or to taste
- 1½ cups peanut oil or melted ghee for deep-frying

Directions:

1. Heat the oil in a big wok or saucepan using moderate to high heat until it achieves 325°F to 350°F on a frying thermometer. (Put a small piece of ginger into the hot oil. If it takes about fifteen to twenty seconds before it rises to the top, the oil is hot enough to proceed with the frying.) Put in the ginger in 1 or 2 batches and fry, stirring and reducing the heat if required, until rich gold in color, three to five minutes per batch.

2. Try to leave behind as much oil as you can in the wok as you take out the ginger using a slotted spoon to a container, toss with salt, and allow to sit until crunchy and cool. Move to an airtight vessel and place in your fridge for a maximum of sixty days.

CRISPY FRIED ONIONS

This recipe is called "Bhuna pyaz" in Hindi

Yield: Approximately 3 cups

These are great for garnish, and a great addition to the curries.

Ingredients:

- 1½ cups peanut oil for deep frying
- 6 to 8 small onions, cut in half along the length and thinly chopped

Directions:

1. Heat the oil in a big wok or saucepan using moderate to high heat until it achieves 325°F to 350°F on a frying thermometer. (Place a small piece of onion into the hot oil. If it takes about fifteen to twenty seconds before it rises to the top, the oil is hot enough to proceed with the frying.) Put in the onions in 1 or 2 batches and fry, stirring and reducing the heat if required, until deep brown, approximately five to seven minutes per batch.
2. Try to leave behind as much oil as you can in the wok as you take out the onions using a slotted spoon to paper towels and allow to sit until crunchy and cool. Move to an airtight vessel and place in your fridge for a maximum of sixty days.

HOMEMADE YOGURT

This recipe is called "Ghar ki dahi" in Hindi

Yield: Approximately 4 cups

If you're buying all your yogurt from a store, you don't know what you're missing out. Fresh homemade yogurt tastes absolutely amazing, is more nutritious, is free of preservatives, and the feeling you get when you make yogurt is great. You just have to do it once to know what I'm talking about.

All you need to make it is some milk and a starter. The starter can be store-bought yogurt with live cultures or yogurt from a prior homemade batch. Depending on your personal taste and diet restrictions, you can choose any kind of milk too.

Ingredients:

- 1 or 2 large, thick kitchen towels
- 1 pot holder
- 2 tablespoons plain yogurt, non-fat or any kind, with active culture
- 4 cups milk

Directions:

1. Bring the milk to a boil, stirring regularly using a metal spatula in a heavy aluminium saucepan to avoid burning the milk. You can also do this using a microwave.
2. Move to a yogurt pot (if possible ceramic, though any vessel will do), and cool until the milk registers 118°F to 120°F on a thermometer.
3. Mix in the yogurt starter and cover loosely using a loosely fitting lid.
4. Place a pot holder on a shelf in a kitchen cabinet. Put the yogurt pot on top of the pot holder, fold the towels in half and cover the yogurt pot tightly on every side. This insulates the pot and helps maintain the perfect temperature essential for the proliferation of the yogurt bacteria. You can achieve the same result by placing the yogurt pot in a deactivated gas oven using a small pilot light.
5. Let the milk rest without interruption for three to four hours.
6. Remove the lid and see if the yogurt is firm—kind of like gelatin. If you see a layer of water over the yogurt, let is be for now. You can remove it after chilling. Once the yogurt is set, place it in your fridge instantly. If you allow yogurt to sit at room temperature for too long, it will develop a sour taste.

INDIAN CLARIFIED BUTTER

This recipe is called "Ghee" in Hindi

Ghee is a class of clarified butter that originated in ancient India. It is commonly used in cuisine of the Indian subcontinent, Middle Eastern cuisine, Southeast Asian cuisine, traditional medicine, and religious rituals. Ghee has an amazing fragrance, and red chilli powder fried in ghee has an aroma out of this world. Try it out! Although delicious, it is pure fat, so use in moderation. It is easily available online and in grocery stores, but you can also make your own. Here's how:

Yield: Approximately 2 cups

Ingredients:

- 1 pound unsalted butter
- One 1-foot-square piece of fine muslin or 4 layers of cheesecloth

Directions:

1. Put the butter in a heavy, moderate-sized saucepan and simmer, stirring intermittently, using moderate to low heat until the milk solids turn golden and settle to the bottom of the pan, 15 to 20 minutes. Initially the butter will start to froth, but as it simmers, the foaming will settle. After this, pass everything through the cheesecloth or a fine-mesh strainer into a sanitized jar.
2. Do not throw away the leftover milk solids. Store them at room temperature around two days or in the fridge for approximately six months. Or mix with whole-wheat flour to make paranthas (griddle-fried breads) or add to soups, rice, and steamed vegetables for flavour.

Feel free to add any or all of the following ingredients into the ghee to tweak its flavour.

- ¼ cup minced fresh mint leaves
- ½ cup minced fresh curry leaves plus ¼ teaspoon ground asafoetida
- 1 tablespoon crudely chopped garlic
- 1 teaspoon black peppercorns and 1 teaspoon ajwain seeds
- 1 teaspoon dried fenugreek leaves
- 2 tablespoons peeled and minced fresh ginger
- 2 teaspoons cumin seeds, 2 black cardamom pods, crushed lightly to break the skin, and 2 (1-inch) sticks cinnamon

PANEER CHEESE

This recipe is called "Paneer" in Hindi

Yield: 8 ounces or approximately 30 1¼-inch pieces

Basically, this is Indian cottage cheese. It is easily available in Indian markets, and is one of the most delicious ingredients vegetarians get to enjoy. You can easily make this at home. Here's how:

Ingredients:

- ½ gallon lowfat or whole milk
- 1 (2-foot-square) piece of fine muslin or 4 layers of cheesecloth
- 2 cups plain yogurt, non-fat or any kind, whisked until the desired smoothness is achieved, or ¼ cup fresh lemon juice, or a mixture of both

Directions:

1. Put the milk in a big and heavy saucepan and bring to a boil, stirring slowly, using high heat. Before the milk boils and the bubbles spill over, stir in the yogurt or the lemon juice, and carry on stirring until the milk curdles and separates into curds and whey, approximately a minute or two. Turn off the heat.
2. Cover a big pan using the muslin or cheesecloth and pour the curdled milk over it. The whey should drain through the cloth into the pan, and the curdled paneer cheese is left behind in the cloth.
3. While the paneer cheese is still inside it, pick up the cloth from the pan and fasten the ends of the cloth around the kitchen faucet to drain, ensuring that the cheese is a few inches over the bottom of the sink. let drain three to five minutes.
4. Take out of the faucet and carefully twist the cloth tightly around the cheese, then place the cheese between two salad-size plates (or any other flat surfaces), with the fastened cloth edges placed to one side, out of the way. Put a big pan of water on the top plate and allow the cheese to drain further, approximately ten to twelve minutes.
5. Take paneer cheese out, cut into shapes and sizes you want and use as required. Store in an airtight vessel in the fridge 4 to five days or freeze for no more than 4 months.

YOGURT CHEESE

This recipe is called "Dahi ka paneer" in Hindi

Yield: Approximately 2 cups

Yogurt cheese is basically highly condensed, almost cheese-like yogurt. Here's how we do it:

Ingredients:

- 1 (2-foot-square) piece of fine muslin or 4 layers of cheesecloth
- 1 (32-ounce) vessel non-fat plain yogurt

Directions:

1. Put yogurt in the muslin or cheesecloth, then twist the cloth tightly around the cheese and tie the ends of the cloth around the kitchen faucet, ensuring that the yogurt is a few inches above the bottom of the sink. let drain 4 to 6 hours. The cheese is now ready to be used.
2. Or, set a large colander or fine-mesh strainer into a large container (to catch the whey), and line it with muslin or 4 layers of cheesecloth. Put the yogurt in the strainer and let drain for four to six hours in a fridge.

BASIC SPICE BLENDS

Getting the seasoning right is a vital component of Indian cooking. You can buy readymade Indian spice blends in the market, and these are usually high in quality and taste. As a beginner, feel free to buy readymade spice blends. As you start to become more proficient in Indian cooking, however, you yourself will desire more control over how the final recipe tastes. You cannot tweak the amount of salt in a readymade curry powder, but if you make your own, the possibilities are endless.

So, in this section, we will take a look at a few of the most extensively used Indian spice blends. We will learn the basic ingredients used in them, and the directions you will need to follow to make these at your home. Once you get used to making these basic spice blends, feel free to play around and create your own spice blends, tailored exactly to your and your family's tastes!

CURRY POWDERS

Curries are the quintessence of Indian food. Curries are usually a blend of wet and dry ingredients. Wet ingredients are usually ground juicy ingredients like tomatoes, ginger, onions, etc. The dried ingredients are the spices, herbs, nuts, etc. These dry ingredients are the primary tastemakers, and we will take a look at these in this section.

BASIC CURRY POWDER (V)

This recipe is called "Kari ka masala" in Hindi

Yield: Approximately 1½ cups

Buy this from a local Indian store, or online. However, it is more fun to make your own!

Ingredients:

- ⅓ cup ground cumin seeds
- 1 cup ground coriander seeds
- 1 tablespoon ground cayenne pepper (not compulsory)
- 1 tablespoon ground dried fenugreek leaves
- 1 tablespoon ground paprika
- 2 tablespoons ground turmeric

Directions:

1. Add all the spices to a container and stir using a spoon until they get blended.
2. Put inside an airtight vessel and place the vessel in a cool, dark place, approximately thirty days at room temperature or approximately one year in a fridge.

SPICED BASIC CURRY POWDER (V)

This recipe is called "Kari ka masala" in Hindi

Yield: Approximately 2 cups

Basic curry powder we saw above, but with some extra flavour.

Ingredients:

- *1 recipe* Basic Curry Powder
- 1 tablespoon ground black cardamom seeds
- 1 tablespoon ground black peppercorns
- 1 tablespoon ground dried ginger
- 1 tablespoon ground fennel seeds
- 1 tablespoon ground fenugreek seeds
- 1 tablespoon ground green cardamom seeds
- 1 teaspoon ground cinnamon
- 1 teaspoon ground cloves
- 1 teaspoon ground nutmeg

Directions:

1. Add all the spices to a container and stir using a spoon until they get blended.
2. Put inside an airtight vessel and place the vessel in a cool, dark place, approximately thirty days at room temperature or approximately one year in a fridge.

GOAN CURRY POWDER

This recipe is called "Goa ka shakuti masala" in Hindi

Yield: Approximately 1½ cups

This Goan tastemaker goes perfectly with meat and chicken!

Ingredients:

- ¼ cup coriander seeds
- ¼ cup thinly chopped fresh garlic cloves
- ¾ cup grated fresh or frozen coconut or shredded unsweetened dried coconut
- 1 2-inch stick cinnamon, broken
- 1 tablespoon black peppercorns
- 1 tablespoon cumin seeds
- 1 teaspoon ajwain seeds
- 1 teaspoon black cumin seeds
- 1 teaspoon fennel seeds

- 1 teaspoon ground nutmeg
- 1 teaspoon ground turmeric
- 10 whole cloves
- 15 dried red chile peppers, such as chile de arbol, broken
- 2 tablespoons white poppy seeds
- 3 to 5 fresh green chile peppers, such as serrano, thinly chopped
- 8 to 10 green cardamom pods, lightly crushed to break the skin
- 8 to 10 quarter-size slices of peeled fresh ginger
- 8 to 10 star anise, broken

Directions:

1. In a moderate-sized cast-iron or non-stick wok or skillet, roast the coconut, stirring and shaking the skillet using moderate to low heat, until the coconut is crunchy and golden, approximately eight to ten minutes. If the coconut is not crunchy after ten minutes, reduce the heat further to prevent browning, and cautiously watch for the next few minutes until the coconut becomes crunchy. Move to a container.
2. In the same skillet, place the garlic, ginger, and green chile peppers and dry-roast, stirring and swaying the pan using low heat until most of the moisture evaporates and the mixture is golden, approximately eight to ten minutes. Put into the coconut.
3. Put the rest of the spices in the skillet and dry-roast using moderate to low heat, stirring and swaying the pan until a golden colour is achieved and highly fragrant, approximately eight to ten minutes. Allow to cool, mix all ingredients together, and grind using a spice or coffee grinder till you get a fine powder. Store in an airtight vessel about three months in the fridge or approximately one year in the freezer.

GUJARATI CURRY POWDER Ⓥ

This recipe is called "Dhana-jeera masala" in Hindi

Yield: Approximately 1¼ cups

A classic curry powder from North-West India!

Ingredients:

- ¼ cup cumin seeds
- 1 cup coriander seeds
- 1 tablespoon cayenne pepper

Directions:

1. In a moderate-sized cast-iron or non-stick skillet, roast the cumin seeds, stirring and swaying the pan over moderate heat until smoke with a strong fragrance starts to rise and the seeds appear slightly darker, approximately two to three minutes. Put in the coriander seeds and roast until they are just heated through, approximately one minute.
2. Allow to cool, then grind using a spice or a coffee grinder till you get a fine powder. Move the mixture to a container and stir in the cayenne pepper. Put inside an airtight vessel and place the vessel in a cool, dark place, approximately thirty days at room temperature or approximately one year in a fridge.

KASHMIRI CURRY POWDER (V)

This recipe is called "Kashmiri kari ka masala" in Hindi

Yield: Approximately 2 cups

A tastemaker from the Icy state of Kashmir in North India.

Ingredients:

- ¼ cup cumin seeds
- ¼ cup fenugreek seeds
- ½ cup fennel seeds
- 1 tablespoon ground paprika
- 1 teaspoon ground cloves
- 1 teaspoon ground mace
- 1 teaspoon ground nutmeg
- 1 teaspoon saffron threads
- 10 bay leaves, crudely broken
- 2 tablespoons black cardamom seeds
- 2 tablespoons green cardamom seeds
- 2 tablespoons mustard or vegetable oil
- 2 teaspoons ground cinnamon

- 3 tablespoons ground ginger
- 4 to 5 large cloves fresh garlic, minced
- 8 to 12 dried red chile peppers, such as chile de arbol, broken

Directions:

1. In a moderate-sized cast-iron or non-stick wok or skillet, heat the oil over moderate heat and stir the red chile peppers and garlic until a golden colour is achieved, approximately one minute. Put in the fennel, cumin, fenugreek, black and green cardamom, bay leaves, and saffron, and roast, stirring and swaying the pan, until the mixture becomes slightly darker, approximately two minutes.
2. Allow to cool, then grind using a spice or coffee grinder to make a very fine powder. Put in a container and stir in the ginger, paprika, cinnamon, cloves, mace, and nutmeg. Put inside an airtight vessel and place the vessel in a cool, dark place, approximately seven days at room temperature or approximately one year in a fridge.

MARATHI CURRY POWDER Ⓥ

This recipe is called "Goda masala" in Hindi

Yield: Approximately 2 cups

A delicious curry powder from Maharashtra and Bombay, the home to Bollywood!

Ingredients:

- ¼ cup cumin seeds
- ¼ cup shredded unsweetened dried coconut
- ¼ cup white sesame seeds
- 1 cup coriander seeds
- 1 tablespoon cayenne pepper
- 1 tablespoon salt, or to taste
- 1 teaspoon black cumin seeds
- 1 teaspoon ground asafoetida
- 1 teaspoon ground turmeric
- 2 tablespoons black mustard seeds

Directions:

1. In a moderate-sized cast-iron or non-stick skillet, roast the coconut, coriander seeds, cumin seeds, white sesame seeds, black mustard seeds, and black cumin seeds, stirring constantly, initially over high and then over moderate heat until a golden colour is achieved and fragrant, approximately two to three minutes. Allow to cool, then grind using a spice or coffee grinder till you get a fine powder.
2. Put back into the skillet, stir in the cayenne pepper, salt, turmeric, and asafoetida, and stir over moderate heat until heated through, approximately one minute. Allow to cool completely and put inside an airtight vessel and place the vessel in a cool, dark place, approximately thirty days at room temperature or approximately one year in a fridge.

SOUTH INDIAN CURRY POWDER Ⓥ

This recipe is called "Kootupodi" in Hindi

Yield: Approximately 2 cups

This curry powder has a mild aroma that enhances flavour, and is great for thickening those curries and soups.

Ingredients:

- ¼ cup dried white urad beans (dhulli urad dal), sorted
- ¼ cup fenugreek seeds
- ½ cup coriander seeds
- 1 cup parboiled (converted) rice
- 10 to 12 dried red chile peppers, such as chile de arbol, broken

Directions:

1. In a moderate-sized cast-iron or non-stick skillet, roast the rice, dal, fenugreek seeds, and red chile peppers using moderate to low heat, stirring until a golden colour is achieved, approximately ten minutes. Stir in the coriander seeds and stir until heated through.
2. Allow to cool and grind using a spice or coffee grinder till you get a powder. Put inside an airtight vessel and place the vessel in a cool, dark place, approximately thirty days at room temperature or approximately one year in a fridge.

GARAM MASALAS

BASIC GARAM MASALA Ⓥ

This recipe is called "Garam masala" in Hindi

Yield: Approximately 1½ cups

"Garam" means hot in Hindi, and "Masala" means spice. So, as the name suggests, Garam Masalas are spicy hot blends, and are easily one of the most common tastemakers in India. There are many versions of this available all through India. These are easily available in stores, or you can buy them on amazon. But if you want a version that suits your personal taste, learn to make your own!

Ingredients:

- ¼ cup ground black cardamom seeds
- ¼ cup ground cloves
- ⅓ cup ground cinnamon
- ⅓ cup ground freshly black pepper
- 3 tablespoons ground green cardamom seeds

Directions:

1. In a moderate-sized cast-iron or non-stick skillet, mix and roast all the spices, stirring and swaying the pan over moderate heat until heated through, approximately two minutes.
2. Allow to cool, then put inside an airtight vessel and place the vessel in a cool, dark place, approximately thirty days at room temperature or approximately one year in a fridge.

HYDERABADI GARAM MASALA Ⓥ

This recipe is called "Hyderabad ka garam masala" in Hindi

Yield: Approximately 1½ cups

If the basic garam masala doesn't do it for you, and you want something even stronger and spicier, try this one!

Ingredients:

- ¼ cup freshly ground black pepper
- ¼ cup ground black cumin seeds
- ¼ cup ground cinnamon
- ¼ cup ground cloves
- ¼ cup ground green cardamom seeds
- 2 teaspoons saffron threads dry-roasted and ground

Directions:

1. Dry-roast and grind the saffron before you begin. Next, in a moderate-sized cast-iron or non-stick skillet, mix and roast all the spices, stirring and swaying the pan over moderate heat until heated through, approximately two minutes.
2. Allow to cool, then put inside an airtight vessel and place the vessel in a cool, dark place, approximately thirty days at room temperature or approximately one year in a fridge.

KASHMIRI GARAM MASALA (V)

This recipe is called "Kashmir ka garam masala" in Hindi

Yield: 1½ cups

A version of garam masala from the icy peaks of North India. Highly rich and fragrant, this version goes great with non-vegetarian dishes.

Ingredients:

- ¼ cup black cumin seeds
- ¼ cup black peppercorns
- ½ cup fennel seeds
- 1 tablespoon ground cinnamon
- 1 tablespoon ground cloves
- 1 tablespoon ground ginger
- 1 teaspoon ground mace
- 1 teaspoon ground nutmeg

- 1 teaspoon saffron threads
- 2 tablespoons green cardamom seeds

Directions:

1. In a moderate-sized cast-iron or non-stick skillet, mix and roast the fennel and cumin seeds, peppercorns, cardamom seeds, and saffron threads, stirring and swaying the pan over moderate heat until heated through, approximately two minutes.
2. Allow to cool, then grind using a spice or coffee grinder till you get a fine powder. Move to a container and stir in the cinnamon, ginger, cloves, mace, and nutmeg. Move the mixture back to the skillet and roast using moderate heat until heated through once more. Allow to cool, then put inside an airtight vessel and place the vessel in a cool, dark place about thirty days at room temperature or approximately one year in a fridge.

MUGHLAI GARAM MASALA (V)

This recipe is called "Mughlai garam masala" in Hindi

Yield: Approximately 1½ cups

This version of the garam masala was brought to India by the Mughals, Muslim dynasts who ruled India for more than 300 years!

Ingredients:

- ¼ cup freshly ground black pepper
- ¼ cup ground cumin seeds
- 1 tablespoon ground bay leaves
- 1 tablespoon saffron threads, dry-roasted and ground
- 1 teaspoon ground mace
- 1 teaspoon ground nutmeg
- 2 tablespoons ground black cardamom seeds
- 2 tablespoons ground black cumin seeds
- 2 tablespoons ground cinnamon
- 2 tablespoons ground cloves
- 2 tablespoons ground ginger
- 2 tablespoons ground green cardamom seeds

Directions:

1. Ready the saffron. Next, in a moderate-sized cast-iron or non-stick skillet, roast all the spices together, stirring and swaying the pan over moderate heat until heated through, approximately two minutes.
2. Allow to cool, then put inside an airtight vessel and place the vessel in a cool, dark place, approximately thirty days at room temperature or approximately one year in a fridge.

PARSI GARAM MASALA Ⓥ

This recipe is called "Parsi garam masala" in Hindi

Yield: Approximately 1½ cups

Parsis migrated to India from Iran, and their version of the garam masala goes perfectly with meat dishes!

Ingredients:

- ¼ cup ground black peppercorns
- ¼ cup ground cinnamon
- ¼ cup ground cumin
- ⅓ cup ground green cardamom seeds
- 2 tablespoons ground cloves
- 3 tablespoons ground star anise

Directions:

1. In a moderate-sized cast-iron or non-stick skillet, mix and roast all the spices, stirring and swaying the pan over moderate heat until heated through, approximately two minutes.
2. Allow to cool, then put inside an airtight vessel and place the vessel in a cool, dark place, approximately thirty days at room temperature or approximately one year in a fridge.

SAVORY SPICE BLENDS

CHAAT MASALA Ⓥ

This recipe is called "Chaat masala" in Hindi

Yield: Approximately 1½ cups

Chaat or chat is a savoury and spicy snack that originated in India, typically served at roadside tracks from stalls or food carts across the Indian subcontinent in India.

Ingredients:

- ¼ cup mango powder
- ⅓ tablespoons cumin seeds, dry-roasted and ground
- 1 tablespoon citric acid
- 1 tablespoon ground black salt
- 1 teaspoon ground asafoetida
- 1 to 2 tablespoons salt, or to taste
- 1 to 3 teaspoons cayenne pepper, or to taste
- 2 tablespoons ground ajwain seeds
- 2 tablespoons ground ginger
- 2 tablespoons tamarind powder
- 3 tablespoons dried mint leaves, ground

Directions:

1. Ready the cumin seeds. Next, in a moderate-sized cast-iron or non-stick skillet, mix and roast all the spices, stirring and swaying the pan over moderate heat until heated through, approximately two minutes.
2. Allow to cool, then put inside an airtight vessel and place the vessel in a cool, dark place, approximately thirty days at room temperature or approximately one year in a fridge.

NEW DELHI STREET FOOD MASALA Ⓥ

This recipe is called "Papri chaat masala" in Hindi

Yield: 1½ cups

A taste of from streets of the capital of India.

Ingredients:

- ½ cup cumin seeds
- 1 tablespoon ajwain seeds
- 1 tablespoon cayenne pepper, or to taste
- 1 tablespoon ground black salt
- 1 tablespoon ground ginger
- 1 tablespoon salt, or to taste
- 3 tablespoons ground dried mint leaves
- 3 tablespoons mango powder
- 3 tablespoons tamarind powder

Directions:

1. In a moderate-sized cast-iron or non-stick skillet, mix and roast the cumin and ajwain seeds, stirring and swaying the pan over moderate heat until the spices are seems slightly darker, approximately two minutes. Move to a container.
2. Allow to cool, then grind using a spice or coffee grinder till you get a fine powder. Return the mixture to the skillet and Put in the mango and tamarind powder, mint leaves, ginger, black salt, salt, and cayenne pepper.
3. Roast once again over moderate heat until heated through, approximately one minute. Allow to cool, then put inside an airtight vessel and place the vessel in a cool, dark place, approximately thirty days at room temperature or approximately one year in a fridge.

BOMBAY BREAD-SNACK MASALA Ⓥ

This recipe is called "Pav-bhaji ka masala" in Hindi

Yield: Approximately 1½ cups

This one is from the streets of Mumbai.

Ingredients:

- ⅓ cup ground coriander seeds
- ⅓ cup ground cumin
- ½ cup freshly ground black pepper
- 1 to 2 tablespoons cayenne pepper, or to taste
- 1½ teaspoons ground asafoetida

- 1½ teaspoons ground black cardamom seeds
- 1½ teaspoons ground cinnamon
- 1½ teaspoons ground cloves
- 1½ teaspoons ground turmeric

Directions:

1. In a moderate-sized cast-iron or non-stick skillet, roast all the spices, stirring and shaking the skillet over moderate heat, until the mixture is fragrant and golden, approximately two minutes.
2. Allow to cool, then put inside an airtight vessel and place the vessel in a cool, dark place, approximately thirty days at room temperature or approximately one year in a fridge.

CUMIN-WATER MASALA Ⓥ

This recipe is called "Jeera paani masala" in Hindi

Yield: 1½ cups

This powder is commonly enjoyed mixed with water, but it can also be used as a tastemaker for various recipes.

Ingredients:

- ¼ cup ground dried mint leaves
- ⅓ cup cumin seeds
- ½ cup dried mango or tamarind powder, sifted
- 1 tablespoon black cumin seeds
- 1 tablespoon ground ginger
- 1 tablespoon salt, or to taste
- 1 teaspoon dried cayenne pepper, or to taste
- 1 teaspoon freshly ground black pepper, or to taste
- 1 teaspoon ground asafoetida
- 1 teaspoon vegetable oil
- 2 teaspoons ajwain seeds
- 2 teaspoons ground black salt

Directions:

1. In a moderate-sized cast-iron or non-stick wok or skillet, mix and roast the cumin seeds, black cumin seeds, and ajwain seeds, stirring and swaying the pan over moderate heat until heated through, approximately two minutes. Take the skillet off the heat. Allow to cool, then grind using a spice or coffee grinder till you get a fine powder.
2. Heat the oil in a small non-stick saucepan using moderate to high heat and Put in the asafoetida. It will sizzle upon contact with the hot oil. Swiftly put in the ground spice mixture and all the rest of the spices. Mix thoroughly and stir until heated through, approximately two minutes. Allow to cool, then put inside an airtight vessel and place the vessel in a cool, dark place, approximately thirty days at room temperature or approximately one year in a fridge.

GRIDDLE-FRIED BREAD MASALA Ⓥ

This recipe is called "Parantha masala" in Hindi

Yield: 1½ cups

Sprinkle this masala over griddle-fried breads or "paranthas".

Ingredients:

- ¼ cup ajwain seeds, crudely ground
- ⅓ cup black peppercorns, crudely ground
- ⅓ cup ground dried fenugreek leaves
- ⅓ cup ground dried mint leaves
- 1 tablespoon black salt (not compulsory)
- 1 tablespoon salt, or to taste

Directions:

1. In a small-sized container, combine all the spices using a spoon.
2. Put inside an airtight vessel and place the vessel in a cool, dry place, approximately thirty days at room temperature or approximately one year in a fridge.

STUFFED GRIDDLE-FRIED BREAD MASALA Ⓥ

This recipe is called "Bharvaan parantha ka masala" in Hindi

Yield: 1½ cups

Ingredients:

- ¼ cup ground dried pomegranate seeds
- ½ cup ground coriander seeds
- 1 tablespoon black salt
- 1 tablespoon cayenne pepper
- 1 tablespoon garam masala
- 1 tablespoon ground ginger
- 1 tablespoon salt, or to taste
- 1 teaspoon ground mace
- 1 teaspoon ground nutmeg
- 2 tablespoons ajwain seeds, crudely ground
- 2 tablespoons ground dried mint leaves
- 2 tablespoons mango powder

Directions:

1. In a small-sized container, combine all the spices using a spoon.
2. Put inside an airtight vessel and place the vessel in a cool, dry place, approximately thirty days at room temperature or approximately one year in a fridge.

ROASTED CHILE PEPPER AND RED PEPPERCORN MASALA
Ⓥ

This recipe is called "Bhuna mirchi ka masala" in Hindi

Yield: Approximately ½ cup

This one is probably the hottest masala in this book. Use carefully.

Ingredients:

- 1 tablespoon vegetable oil
- 1 teaspoon salt, or to taste
- 15 to 20 dried red chile peppers, such as chile de arbol, broken

- 2 tablespoons red peppercorns
- 2 to 4 tablespoons ground paprika

Directions:

1. In a moderate-sized cast-iron or non-stick wok or skillet, heat the oil over moderate heat and roast the chile peppers, stirring and swaying the pan, until crunchy and seems slightly darker, approximately a minute or two. This will cause a lot of irritating smoke, so do this outdoors if possible, or when you you're alone in the house, and are willing to suffer a little by yourself. Move to a container.
2. Put in the red peppercorns and roast until heated through, without browning them. Put into the chile peppers. Allow to cool, then grind using a spice or coffee grinder till you get a fine powder. Stir in the paprika and salt and put inside an airtight vessel and place the vessel in a cool, dark place, approximately thirty days at room temperature or approximately one year in a fridge.

ROASTED CUMIN AND FENUGREEK MASALA Ⓥ

This recipe is called "Bhuna jeera aur methi ka masala" in Hindi

Yield: Approximately 1 cup

This one goes great in sauces!

Ingredients:

- ¼ cup cumin seeds
- 1 teaspoon ground turmeric
- 12 to 15 dried red chile peppers, such as chile de arbol, broken
- 2 tablespoons fenugreek seeds
- 2 teaspoons salt, or to taste

Directions:

1. In a moderate-sized cast-iron or non-stick skillet, mix and roast the cumin seeds, fenugreek seeds, and red chile peppers over moderate heat, stirring and swaying the pan until seems slightly darker and highly fragrant, approximately two minutes.

2. Allow to cool, then grind using a spice or coffee grinder till you get a fine powder. Stir in the salt and turmeric and put inside an airtight vessel and place the vessel in a cool, dark place, approximately thirty days at room temperature or approximately one year in a fridge.

ROASTED CUMIN-PEPPER MASALA ⓥ

This recipe is called "Bhuna jeera aur kaali-mirch ka masala" in Hindi

Yield: ½ cup

This one goes great with yogurt and salads.

Ingredients:

- ¼ cup cumin seeds
- 1 tablespoon hot red pepper flakes, or to taste
- 3 tablespoons black peppercorns

Directions:

1. In a small-sized cast-iron or non-stick skillet, roast separately the cumin seeds, the peppercorns, and the red pepper flakes, over moderate heat, stirring and swaying the pan until fragrant and seems slightly darker, approximately two minutes each for the cumin and the peppercorns, and just a few seconds for the red chile flakes.
2. Combine the roasted cumin, peppercorns and red pepper flakes. Allow to cool, then put in your pepper mill. Grind and use as needed. Or, grind crudely using a spice of coffee grinder, put inside an airtight vessel and place the vessel in a cool, dark place, approximately thirty days at room temperature or approximately one year in a fridge.

PUNJABI RAITA AND BUTTERMILK MASALA ⓥ

This recipe is called "Punjabi raita aur lussi ka masala" in Hindi

Yield: Approximately ⅓ cup

Ingredients:

- ¼ cup cumin seeds, dry-roasted and crudely ground
- 1 tablespoon black peppercorns, dry-roasted and crudely ground
- 1 tablespoon crudely ground dried mint leaves
- 1 teaspoon ground paprika
- 1 teaspoon salt, or to taste

Directions:

1. In a container, combine all the spices using a spoon.
2. Put inside an airtight vessel and place the vessel in a cool, dry place, approximately thirty days at room temperature or approximately one year in a fridge.

KASHMIRI RAITA MASALA Ⓥ

This recipe is called "Kashmir ka raita masala" in Hindi

Yield: Approximately ½ cup

Ingredients:

- ¼ cup coriander seeds
- ½ to 1 teaspoon cayenne pepper
- 1 tablespoon black mustard seeds
- 1 teaspoon salt, or to taste
- 2 rice-size pieces asafoetida
- 2 tablespoons cumin seeds
- 2 tablespoons fennel seeds
- 2 teaspoons ground ginger

Directions:

1. In a moderate-sized cast-iron or non-stick skillet, mix and roast the coriander seeds, and fennel seeds and cumin seeds, stirring and swaying the pan over moderate heat until heated through, approximately two minutes. Move to a container.
2. In the same skillet, dry-roast the asafoetida and the mustard seeds until they begin to pop, approximately one minute. (Cover pan momentarily to contain popping, if required.) Combine with the coriander-fennel-cumin mixture.

3. Allow to cool, then grind using a spice or coffee grinder till you get a fine powder. Stir in the ginger, cayenne pepper, and salt. Put inside an airtight vessel and place the vessel in a cool, dark place, approximately thirty days at room temperature or approximately one year in a fridge.

MASALA BLENDS FOR SPECIAL DISHES

BENGALI FIVE WHOLE SPICE BLEND Ⓥ

This recipe is called "Panch-phoran" in Hindi

Yield: Approximately 1½ cups

A delicious blend of five spices popular in east India that goes great with non-vegetarian curries and dishes.

Ingredients:

- ¼ cup black mustard seeds
- ⅓ cup fennel seeds
- ⅔ cup cumin seeds
- 2 tablespoons fenugreek seeds
- 3 tablespoons kalonji seeds

Directions:

1. In a moderate-sized cast-iron or non-stick wok or skillet, roast all the ingredients together, shaking and stirring the pan using moderate to high heat, until heated through, approximately two minutes.
2. Allow to cool, then put inside an airtight vessel and place the vessel in a cool, dark place, thirty days at room temperature or approximately one year in a fridge.

BRAISED MEAT MASALA Ⓥ

This recipe is called "Korma masala" in Hindi

Yield: Approximately 1½ cups

Typically used for cooking delicious "korma", which means meat braised with yogurt.

Ingredients:

- ¼ cup each: shelled and finely ground raw pistachios, almonds, and cashews nuts
- 1 tablespoon ground black cardamom seeds
- 1 tablespoon ground black pepper
- 1 tablespoon ground cinnamon
- 1 teaspoon ground cloves
- 2 tablespoons ground ginger
- 2 tablespoons ground green cardamom seeds
- 2 tablespoons white poppy seeds

Directions:

1. In a moderate-sized cast-iron or non-stick skillet, mix and roast all the ingredients, stirring and swaying the pan over moderate heat until heated through, approximately two minutes.
2. Allow to cool, then put inside an airtight vessel and place the vessel in a cool, dark place, approximately seven days at room temperature or approximately one year in a fridge.

CHICKPEA MASALA (V)

This recipe is called "Channa masala" in Hindi

Yield: Approximately 1½ cups

Used commonly in chickpea dishes and curries, this masala also goes great with meat dishes.

Ingredients:

- ½ cup ground coriander seeds
- ½ cup ground cumin
- ½ teaspoon ground mace
- 1 tablespoon cayenne pepper, or to taste
- 1 tablespoon freshly ground black pepper, or to taste

- 1 tablespoon ground black cardamom seeds
- 1 tablespoon ground black salt
- 1 tablespoon ground dried fenugreek leaves
- 1 teaspoon ground asafoetida
- 1 teaspoon ground cinnamon
- 1 teaspoon ground cloves
- 1 teaspoon ground ginger
- 1 teaspoon ground nutmeg
- 1 teaspoon ground turmeric
- 2 tablespoons ground dried pomegranate seeds
- 2 tablespoons tamarind or mango powder
- 2 teaspoons ground ajwain seeds

Directions:

1. In a moderate-sized cast-iron or non-stick skillet, mix and roast all the ingredients except the coriander, black salt, and turmeric, stirring and swaying the pan over moderate heat until heated through, approximately two minutes. Reduce the heat to low and stir until dark brown and fragrant, approximately three minutes.
2. Turn off the heat and stir in the coriander, black salt, and turmeric. Allow to cool completely, then put inside an airtight vessel and place the vessel in a cool, dark place, approximately thirty days at room temperature or approximately one year in a fridge.

GRILLING MASALA Ⓥ

This recipe is called "Tandoori masala" in Hindi

Yield: Approximately 1½ cups

A delicious tastemaker for pretty much any recipe right off the grill, or right out or a tandoor.

Ingredients:

- ¼ cup ground dried fenugreek leaves
- *1* cup Mughlai Garam Masala
- 1 tablespoon ground paprika
- 1 teaspoon ground turmeric

- 1 to 2 tablespoons cayenne pepper, or to taste
- 2 tablespoons ground fenugreek seeds

Directions:

1. Ready the Mughlai masala. Add all the spices to a container and stir using a spoon until they get blended.
2. Put inside an airtight vessel and place the vessel in a cool and dark place, approximately thirty days at room temperature or approximately one year in a fridge.

GUJRATI MASALA Ⓥ

This recipe is called "Dhansak masala" in Hindi

Yield: Approximately 2½ cups

Typically used with "Dhansak", a cuisine from Gujrat in West India.

Ingredients:

- ¼ cup black peppercorns
- ¼ cup cumin seeds
- ¼ cup dried curry leaves
- ¼ cup dried red chile peppers, such as chile de arbol, broken
- ¼ cup fenugreek seeds
- 1 cup coriander seeds
- 1 tablespoon black cumin seeds
- 1 tablespoon ground cinnamon
- 1 tablespoon ground cloves
- 1 tablespoon mustard seeds
- 1 tablespoon white poppy seeds
- 1 teaspoon ground mace
- 10 bay leaves, crudely broken
- 2 teaspoons ground black cardamom seeds
- 2 teaspoons ground green cardamom seeds
- 2 teaspoons ground nutmeg
- 4 star anise, broken

Directions:

1. In a moderate-sized cast-iron or non-stick skillet, mix and roast the coriander, cumin, black cumin, peppercorns, fenugreek, and chile peppers, stirring and swaying the pan over moderate heat until the mixture is seems slightly darker, approximately two minutes. Stir in the curry leaves, poppy seeds, mustard seeds, anise, and bay leaves and roast another minute. Remove from heat.
2. Allow to cool, then grind using a spice or coffee grinder till you get a fine powder. Stir in the cinnamon, cloves, black and green cardamom seeds, nutmeg, and mace. Put inside an airtight vessel and place the vessel in a cool, dark place, approximately thirty days at room temperature or approximately one year in a fridge.

MEAT MASALA Ⓥ

This recipe is called "Gosht ka masala" in Hindi

Yield: Approximately 1¼ cups

Sprinkle some of this in your meat curries for great taste!

Ingredients:

- ¼ cup shelled raw peanuts, with papery red skin removed
- 1 tablespoon black mustard seeds
- 1 tablespoon coriander seeds
- 1 tablespoon fenugreek seeds
- 1 teaspoon white poppy seeds
- 10 to 15 dried red chile peppers, such as chile de arbol, broken
- 1½ tablespoons sesame seeds
- 2 tablespoons cumin seeds
- 2 tablespoons dried yellow split chickpeas (channa dal), sorted

Directions:

1. In a moderate-sized cast-iron or non-stick skillet, roast the peanuts, stirring and swaying the pan over moderate heat until the mixture is seems slightly darker, approximately one minute.

2. Put in the chile peppers, dal, cumin seeds, and fenugreek seeds and roast until a golden colour is achieved, approximately two to three minutes. Stir in the sesame, coriander, poppy, and mustard seeds and continue to roast until seems slightly darker, approximately two to three minutes. Allow to cool, then grind using a spice or coffee grinder till you get a fine powder. Put inside an airtight vessel and place the vessel in a cool, dark place, approximately seven days at room temperature or approximately one year in a fridge.

VINDALOO MASALA (V)

This recipe is called "Vindaloo ka masala" in Hindi

Yield: Approximately 1½ cups

A delicious tastemaker from the coastal tourist state of Goa!

Ingredients:

- ¼ cup cumin seeds
- ¾ cup coriander seeds
- 1 tablespoon fenugreek seeds
- 1 teaspoon ground black cardamom seeds
- 1 teaspoon ground cinnamon
- 1 teaspoon ground cloves
- 1 teaspoon ground turmeric
- 2 tablespoons black cumin seeds
- 2 tablespoons black peppercorns
- 2 teaspoons mustard seeds
- 4 to 6 dried red chile peppers, such as chile de arbol, broken

Directions:

1. In a moderate-sized cast-iron or non-stick skillet, mix and roast the red chile peppers, coriander, cumin, black cumin, peppercorns, fenugreek, and mustard seeds, stirring and swaying the pan over moderate heat until seems slightly darker, approximately two minutes.
2. Allow to cool, then grind using a spice or coffee grinder till you get a fine powder. Move to a container and stir in the turmeric, cardamom, cloves, and cinnamon. Put inside an airtight vessel and place the vessel in a cool, dark place,

approximately thirty days at room temperature or approximately one year in a fridge.

WOK MASALA ⓥ

This recipe is called "Kadhai masala" in Hindi

Yield: Approximately 1¼ cups

A tastemaker for recipes typically cooked in a wok or "kadhai".

Ingredients:

- ½ cup crudely ground coriander seeds
- 1 tablespoon cayenne pepper
- 1 tablespoon ground dried pomegranate seeds
- 1 tablespoon ground fennel seeds
- 1 tablespoon ground ginger
- 1 tablespoon mango powder
- 1 teaspoon ground black cardamom seeds
- 1 teaspoon ground black salt
- 1 teaspoon ground nutmeg
- 1 teaspoon ground paprika
- 2 tablespoons ground cumin seeds
- 2 tablespoons ground dried fenugreek leaves
- 2 tablespoons ground dried mint leaves

Directions:

1. Add all the spices to a small-sized container and stir using a spoon until they get blended.
2. Put inside an airtight vessel and place the vessel in a cool, dark place, approximately thirty days at room temperature or approximately one year in a fridge.

SPECIAL SOUTH INDIAN BLENDS

SAMBAR MASALA Ⓥ

This recipe is called "Sambar podi" in Hindi

Yield: Approximately 1½ cups

In South India, you will be served "Sambar" with pretty much everything. This spice blend is the lifeblood of Sambar.

Ingredients:

- ¼ cup shredded, unsweetened, dried coconut
- ⅓ cup dried curry leaves
- ½ cup coriander seeds
- 1 tablespoon each: dried yellow split pigeon peas (toor dal), dried yellow split chickpeas (channa dal), dried white urad beans (dhulli urad dal), sorted
- 1 tablespoon sesame or peanut oil
- 1 teaspoon ground asafoetida
- 1 teaspoon ground turmeric
- 10 to 15 dried red chile peppers, such as chile de arbol, broken
- 2 tablespoons fenugreek seeds

Directions:

1. In a moderate-sized cast-iron or non-stick skillet, heat the oil over moderate heat and stir-fry the red chile peppers until seems slightly darker, approximately one minute. Put in the fenugreek seeds, all the dals, and the asafoetida and stir until a golden colour is achieved, approximately two minutes.
2. Mix in the coconut and stir until a golden colour is achieved, approximately two minutes. Then Put in the coriander seeds, curry leaves, and turmeric, and stir until heated through, approximately one minute. Allow to cool, then grind using a spice or coffee grinder till you get a fine powder. Put inside an airtight vessel and place the vessel in a cool, dark place, approximately thirty days at room temperature or about an year in a fridge.

RASAM MASALA Ⓥ

This recipe is called "Rasam podi" in Hindi

Yield: Approximately 1½ cups

Rasam is the second most popular thing in South India, followed by sambar.

Ingredients:

- ¼ cup dried curry leaves
- ½ teaspoon ground turmeric
- ⅔ cup coriander seeds
- 1 tablespoon black mustard seeds
- 1 tablespoon cumin seeds
- 1 tablespoon fenugreek seeds
- 10 to 15 dried red chile peppers, such as chile de arbol, broken
- 2 tablespoons cumin seeds
- 2 tablespoons dried yellow split chickpeas (channa dal), sorted
- 3 tablespoons black peppercorns
- 3 tablespoons dried yellow split pigeon peas (toor dal), sorted
- 4 to 6 rice-size pieces asafoetida

Directions:

1. In a moderate-sized cast-iron or non-stick wok or skillet, mix and roast all the ingredients, stirring and shaking the skillet over moderate heat until it starts to look golden and releases its fragrance, approximately three minutes.
2. Allow to cool, then grind using a spice or coffee grinder till you get a powder. Put inside an airtight vessel and place the vessel in a cool, dark place, thirty days at room temperature or approximately one year in a fridge.

Variation: Mild Rasam Powder can be made by excluding or reducing the number of red chile peppers. The black peppercorns may be reduced in quantity, but do not omit, because they are essential to this blend.

CHUTNEY COCONUT MASALA Ⓥ

This recipe is called "Chutni nariyal podi" in Hindi

Yield: Approximately 1½ cups

Coconut is a staple in the South Indian kitchen, and this recipe can be used to do a lot.

Ingredients:

- ¼ cup crudely ground dried curry leaves
- 1 cup grated fresh or frozen coconut or shredded unsweetened dried coconut
- 1 tablespoon ground jaggery (gur) or dark brown sugar
- 1 teaspoon ground asafoetida
- 1 to 2 tablespoons tamarind powder
- 2 tablespoons each: dried split pigeon peas (toor dal), dried white urad beans (dhulli urad dal), dried yellow split chickpeas (channa dal), sorted
- 6 to 10 dried red chile peppers, such as chile de arbol, broken

Directions:

1. In a moderate-sized cast-iron or non-stick wok or skillet, roast the coconut, all the dals, red chile peppers, and curry leaves over moderate heat, stirring and swaying the pan until a golden colour is achieved, approximately 4 minutes.
2. Put in the asafoetida, stir for about half a minute, and remove from the heat. Stir in the tamarind powder and jaggery. Allow to cool, then grind using a spice or coffee grinder until as fine a powder as possible. Stir in the salt and put inside an airtight vessel and place the vessel in a cool, dark place, approximately seven days at room temperature or approximately one year in a fridge.

LENTIL PASTE Ⓥ

This recipe is called "Dal podi" in Hindi

Yield: Approximately 1½ cups

A delicious spice blend that adds flavour and thickens.

Ingredients:

- ¼ cup dried split pigeon peas (toor dal), sorted
- ¼ cup dried white urad beans (dhulli urad dal), sorted
- ½ cup dried yellow split chickpeas (channa dal), sorted
- ½ teaspoon ground asafoetida
- 1 tablespoon cumin seeds
- 1 tablespoon peanut oil
- 10 to 12 dried red chile peppers, such as chile de arbol, broken
- 2 teaspoons salt, or to taste

Directions:

1. In a moderate-sized cast-iron or non-stick wok or skillet, heat the oil using moderate to high heat and stir-fry the dals, cumin seeds, and red chile peppers until seems slightly darker, approximately two minutes.
2. Put in the asafoetida and stir about 30 seconds. Allow to cool, then grind using a spice or coffee grinder until a fine paste is achieved. Stir in the salt and put inside an airtight vessel and place the vessel in a cool, dark place, thirty days at room temperature or approximately one year in a fridge.

PEANUT MASALA ⓥ

This recipe is called "Moong-phalli or nilakkadala podi" in Hindi

Yield: Approximately 1½ cups

A great seasoning for green salads, chicken, and vegetables!

Ingredients:

- ⅓ cup white sesame seeds, dry-roasted
- 1 cup roasted peanuts, papery skin removed
- 1 teaspoon ground asafoetida
- 1 teaspoon sesame or peanut oil
- 3 to 4 tablespoons dried curry leaves
- 5 to 7 dried red chile peppers, such as chile de arbol, broken

Directions:

1. Ready the sesame seeds. Next, in a moderate-sized cast-iron or non-stick wok or skillet, heat the oil using moderate to high heat and stir-fry the chile peppers until seems slightly darker, approximately one minute. Put in the curry leaves and asafoetida, and stir for about half a minute. Allow to cool, then grind using a spice or coffee grinder till you get a fine powder. Move to a container.
2. Crudely grind the peanuts and sesame seeds using a spice of coffee grinder (you will probably need to do this in 2-3 batches). Put into the ground chile pepper mixture and mix thoroughly. Put inside an airtight vessel and place the vessel in a cool, dark place, approximately seven days at room temperature or approximately one year in a fridge.

SESAME MASALA Ⓥ

This recipe is called "Til or ellu podi" in Hindi

Yield: Approximately 1½ cups

A great garnish for meat and vegetable dishes!

Ingredients:

- 1 tablespoon hot red pepper flakes, or to taste
- 1 teaspoon Asian sesame oil
- 1 teaspoon ground asafoetida
- 1¼ cups white sesame seeds
- 2 tablespoons fenugreek seeds

Directions:

1. In a moderate-sized cast-iron or non-stick wok or skillet, heat the oil using moderate to high heat, put in the fenugreek seeds, red pepper flakes, and asafoetida and stir until a golden colour is achieved, approximately one minute.
2. Put in the sesame seeds, reduce the heat to medium, and roast, stirring and shaking the skillet, until a golden colour is achieved, approximately three minutes. Allow to cool, then grind using a spice or coffee grinder to make as fine a powder as possible. Put inside an airtight vessel and place the vessel in a cool, dark place, approximately seven days at room temperature or about an year in a fridge.

THENGA MASALA Ⓥ

This recipe is called "Thenga podi" in Hindi

Yield: Approximately 1½ cups

A hot and sour tastemaker with an intense flavour.

Ingredients:

- ¼ cup dried white urad beans (dhulli urad dal), sorted
- ¼ cup grated or shredded dried coconut (kopra)

- ¼ cup ground coriander seeds
- ¼ cup ground jaggery (gur) or dark brown sugar
- ¼ teaspoon ground asafoetida
- ½ cup dried yellow split chickpeas (channa dal), sorted
- 1 teaspoon ground turmeric
- 1-inch ball of seedless tamarind pulp, broken into small bits or 1 tablespoon tamarind powder
- 2 teaspoons peanut oil
- 2 teaspoons salt, or to taste
- 7 to 10 dried red chile peppers, such as chile de arbol, broken

Directions:

1. In a moderate-sized cast-iron or non-stick wok or skillet, mix and roast the dals, stirring and shaking the skillet over moderate heat until a golden colour is achieved, approximately two to three minutes. Move to a container.
2. In the same pan, put in the oil and stir-fry the red chile peppers and tamarind until seems slightly darker, approximately two minutes. Move to the container with the roasted dal.
3. Still using the same pan, put in the coriander and coconut and roast until seems slightly darker, two to five minutes. Stir in the jaggery, salt, turmeric, and asafoetida, and roast until the jaggery melts, approximately a minute or two. Stir in the roasted dals, chile peppers and tamarind.
4. Allow to cool, then grind using a spice or coffee grinder until crudely ground. Put inside an airtight vessel and place the vessel in a cool, dark place, approximately three months in the fridge or about an year in the freezer.

DESSERT AND TEA MASALAS

DESSERT MASALA Ⓥ

This recipe is called "Mithai ka masala" in Hindi

Yield: Approximately 1½ cups

This spectacular green powder can be added to pretty much anything sweet to enhance the flavour, and is a great garnish for desserts.

Ingredients:

- ¼ cup cashews, crudely broken
- ½ cup shelled raw almonds, crudely broken
- 1 cup shelled raw pistachios
- 1 tablespoon crudely ground green cardamom seeds
- 1 teaspoon crudely ground black cardamom seeds
- 1 teaspoon saffron threads, dry-roasted and crudely crushed

Directions:

1. Ready the saffron. Next, using a spice grinder or food processor, mix together and pulse the pistachios, almonds, and cashews in one or two batches, until you get a crude powder.
2. Mix in the green and black cardamom seeds and the saffron. Put inside an airtight vessel and store, approximately three months in the fridge or about an year in the freezer.

TEA MASALA Ⓥ

This recipe is called "Chai ka masala" in Hindi

Yield: Approximately 1½ cups

An average Indian adult enjoys tea multiple times per day.

Ingredients:

- ⅓ cup green cardamom seeds
- ½ cup fennel seeds
- 1 tablespoon black peppercorns
- 1 tablespoon ground cinnamon
- 1 tablespoon ground cloves
- 1½ tablespoons ground ginger
- 2 tablespoons black cardamom seeds
- 2 tablespoons dried mint leaves

Directions:

1. Using a spice or coffee grinder, mix together and grind the fennel seeds, green and black cardamom seeds, mint, and peppercorns until a fine powder is achieved.
2. Mix in the ginger, cinnamon, and cloves, and grind one more time to combine the spices. Move to a small vessel and store in a cool, dark place, approximately thirty days at room temperature or approximately one year in a fridge.

BASIC FLAVORING PASTES

BASIC GINGER PASTE Ⓥ

This recipe is called "Pissa adrak" in Hindi

Yield: Approximately 2 cups

Ginger paste is a staple in the Indian kitchen. You can buy this store, but making your own is much more fun.

Ingredients:

- 1 pound fresh ginger, peeled and cut crosswise into thin round slices
- 1 to 3 tablespoons water, as required

Directions:

1. Add the ginger slices to a blender, as you might not get enough smoothness using a food processor. Pulse, pouring in one tablespoon of water at a time, and attain a smooth paste while adding as little water as possible.
2. Move to an airtight vessel and place in your fridge for a maximum of five days or separate into measured batches and freeze about three months. Measured batches can be used directly when you need to cook them.

BASIC GARLIC PASTE Ⓥ

This recipe is called "Pissa lussan" in Hindi

Yield: Approximately 1 cup

Garlic paste is easy to find in markets all over America, but garlic paste that has just been made from fresh garlic will always win.

Ingredients:

- 1½ cups fresh garlic cloves, peeled
- 2 to 3 tablespoons water, as required

Directions:

1. Add the garlic to a blender, as you might not get enough smoothness using a food processor. Pulse, pouring in one tablespoon of water at a time, and attain a smooth paste while adding as little water as possible.
2. Move to an airtight vessel and place in your fridge for a maximum of half a month. Since garlic paste has a strong smell, make sure you thoroughly seal it using plastic wrap below the lid. This will guarantee that the rest of your fridge doesn't smell like garlic. You can also separate into measured batches and freeze about three months. Measured batches used directly when you need to cook them.

ROASTED GARLIC PASTE Ⓥ

This recipe is called "Pissa bhuna lussan" in Hindi

Yield: Approximately 1 cup

Ingredients:

- 1½ cups fresh garlic cloves, peeled

Directions:

1. Heat your oven beforehand to 400°F. Put the garlic cloves in a small pie dish or any other baking pan and roast until a golden brown colour is achieved, approximately fifteen minutes.
2. Allow to cool, then pulse using a blender or crudely mash using a fork. Or just put the roasted cloves in an airtight vessel and place in your fridge for a maximum of

thirty days or freeze for no more than six months. If you don't add any water, puréed roasted garlic can be easily separated even in its frozen form.

BASIC GINGER-GARLIC PASTE Ⓥ

This recipe is called "Pissa adrak-lussan" in Hindi

Yield: Approximately 1½ cups

Probably the most commonly used paste in India, the ginger garlic paste is widely available in stores all over the world. However, the fresh paste you make at home will contain no preservatives and will taste much better! Oil increases the shelf life of this ingredient. Feel free to omit it if you wish to use all of it immediately.

Ingredients:

- 1 cup fresh garlic cloves, peeled
- 1 cup quarter-size slices peeled fresh ginger
- 1 to 3 tablespoons water

Directions:

1. Using a food processor or a blender, combine and pulse the ginger and garlic until a smooth paste is achieved, pouring in water as required for blending.
2. Move to an airtight container, stir in some oil (vegetable, peanut, or olive) until it forms a ⅛-inch layer on top of the paste, and place in your fridge for a maximum of half a month or freeze for no more than six months.

ALMOND AND POPPY SEED PASTE Ⓥ

This recipe is called "Pissa badaam aur khas-khas ka masala" in Hindi

Yield: Approximately 1 cup

Used to make rich, creamy curries.

Ingredients:

- ½ cup shelled raw almonds, crudely chopped
- ½ cup warm water

- ½ cup white poppy seeds
- Seeds from 10 to 15 green cardamom pods

Directions:

1. Immerse the poppy seeds in the water for two hours.
2. Move to a blender, put in the almonds and cardamom seeds, and grind everything until a fine paste is achieved, pouring in additional water if required.
3. Move to an airtight vessel and store in the fridge four days to a week or four months in the freezer.

BASIC CASHEW PASTE Ⓥ

This recipe is called "Pissa kaaju ka masala" in Hindi

Yield: Approximately 1 cup

Great for making rich and thick curries.

Ingredients:

- 1 cup warm water plus more for the paste
- 1¼ cups raw cashews

Directions:

1. Immerse crudely chopped cashews in the warm water to cover, approximately forty five minutes.
2. Drain and pulse using a blender adding 2 to 3 tablespoons water, as required, until a smooth paste is achieved.
3. Move to an airtight vessel and store in the fridge four days to a week or four months in the freezer.

BASIC CURRY PASTE WITH ONION Ⓥ

This recipe is called "Pyaz vaala kari masala" in Hindi

Yield: Approximately ½ cup

A basic curry paste. Feel free to play around and add ingredients you like!

Ingredients:

- ¼ cup peanut oil
- ½ cup crudely chopped fresh cilantro, including soft stems
- 1 large onion, crudely chopped
- 1 to 3 fresh green chile peppers, such as serrano, stemmed
- 2 large tomatoes, crudely chopped
- 3 large cloves fresh garlic, peeled
- 7 to 10 quarter-size slices of peeled fresh ginger

Directions:

1. Using a food processor, process the ginger, garlic, and onion until a smooth paste is achieved. Move to a container. Next, mis together and process the tomatoes, cilantro, and green chile peppers until a smooth purée is achieved.
2. Heat the oil in a big non-stick wok or saucepan using moderate to high heat, put in the ginger-onion paste and cook, using moderate to high heat the first two to three minutes and then over moderate heat until a golden brown colour is achieved, approximately five to seven minutes.
3. Mix in the puréed tomato mixture and cook, stirring until all the liquids vaporize and the oil comes to the sides. Allow to cool and store in an airtight vessel and place in your fridge for a maximum of five days or freeze for no more than three months.

BASIC CURRY PASTE WITHOUT ONION

This recipe is called "Bina pyaz ka kari masala" in Hindi

Yield: Approximately 1 cup

Al alternative to basic curry paste with onion if you don't eat onion,

Ingredients:

- ¼ cup peanut oil
- ¼ cup plain yogurt (non-fat or any kind), whisked until the desired smoothness is achieved
- ½ pound fresh ginger, peeled and thinly chopped
- 1 cup crudely chopped fresh cilantro, including soft stems
- 1 tablespoon cumin seeds

- 2 large tomatoes, crudely chopped
- 5 to 10 fresh green chile peppers, such as serrano, crudely chopped

Directions:

1. Using a food processor, combine and pulse the ginger, chile peppers, cilantro, and tomatoes until a smooth paste is achieved.
2. Heat the oil in a big non-stick wok or saucepan using moderate to high heat and cook the cumin seeds (they should sizzle upon contact with the hot oil). Swiftly put in the paste and cook over moderate heat the first two to three minutes, then using low heat until all the fluids vaporize.
3. Put in the yogurt, slowly and gradually, stirring continuously to stop it from curdling, until all of it is completely blended with the sauce. Allow to cool and store in an airtight vessel about half a month in the fridge or up to three months in the freezer.

BASIC GINGER AND GREEN CHILE PEPPER PASTE Ⓥ

This recipe is called "Pissi hui adrak-hari mirch ka masala" in Hindi

Yield: Approximately 1 cup

This is a decent alternative to ginger-garlic paste. I still prefer ginger-garlic paste though.

Ingredients:

- 10 to 15 fresh green chile peppers, such as serranos, crudely chopped
- 6 ounces fresh ginger, peeled and cut crosswise into thin round slices

Directions:

1. Using a food processor or blender, combine and pulse the ginger and chile peppers to make them as smooth as possible.
2. Move to an airtight vessel and place in your fridge for a maximum of ten days or freeze for no more than 4 months.

BASIC ONION PASTE Ⓥ

This recipe is called "Pyaz ka masala" in Hindi

Yield: Approximately 1 cup

A very commonly used paste in Indian cooking.

Ingredients:

- 1 large onion, crudely chopped (about 8 ounces)
- 10 to 12 quarter-size slices of peeled fresh ginger
- 2 tablespoons water
- 3 to 5 fresh green chile peppers, such as serrano, crudely chopped
- 4 large cloves fresh garlic, peeled

Directions:

1. Add to your blender the water, ginger, and garlic and pulse until the desired smoothness is achieved. Then Put in the onion and process again until the desired smoothness is achieved.
2. Move to an airtight vessel and place in your fridge for a maximum of ten days or freeze for no more than three months.

BOILED ONION PASTE Ⓥ

This recipe is called "Ublae pyaz ka masala" in Hindi

Yield: Approximately 1½ cups

This paste is great for making curries with a smooth texture.

Ingredients:

- ½ cup water
- 1 (1-inch) stick cinnamon, broken along the length into 2 pieces
- 1¼ pounds onions, crudely chopped
- 2 black cardamom pods, pounded lightly to break the skin
- 3 bay leaves
- 4 whole cloves

Directions:

1. Put all the ingredients in a moderate-sized non-stick saucepan. Cover and bring to a boil using moderate to high heat. Reduce the heat to medium-low and simmer until all the water evaporates and the onions are soft, approximately fifteen minutes.
2. Throw away the whole spices, then process the onions using a blender or a food processor until high smoothness is achieved. Move to an airtight vessel and place in your fridge for a maximum of five days or freeze for no more than three months.

CHILE PEPPER PASTE Ⓥ

This recipe is called "Pissi mirchon ka masala" in Hindi

Yield: Approximately ⅓ cup

This one is for the lovers of chile, who enjoy it when their tongue burns and eyes turn red.

Ingredients:

- ¼ cup distilled white vinegar or water
- 10 dried red chile peppers, such as chile de arbol, broken
- 2 teaspoons black peppercorns, dry-roasted and crudely ground
- 5 fresh green chile peppers, such as serrano, crudely chopped

Directions:

1. Immerse the red chile peppers in the vinegar approximately one hour to soften. Move to a blender.
2. Add the green chile peppers and the peppercorns and pulse until the desired smoothness is achieved. Move to an airtight jar and place in your fridge for a maximum of six months.

FRIED ONION PASTE

This recipe is called "Talae pyaz ka masala" in Hindi

Yield: Approximately 1 cup

This paste is used to make delicious rich-tasting curries.

Ingredients:

- ½ cup non-fat plain yogurt
- 1 cup melted ghee or vegetable oil for deep-frying
- 1 large onion, cut in half along the length and thinly chopped
- 4 large cloves fresh garlic, peeled
- 6 to 8 quarter-size slices of peeled fresh ginger

Directions:

1. Heat the oil in a big non-stick saucepan using moderate to high heat and fry the ginger and garlic until a golden colour is achieved, approximately two minutes. Put in the onion and fry until everything is thoroughly browned, approximately five minutes. Place on top of paper towels to drain and save the ghee/oil for future use.
2. Move to a blender or a food processor, put in the yogurt and pulse until a smooth and thick paste is achieved. Move to an airtight vessel and place in your fridge for a maximum of five days or freeze for no more than three months.

GOAN VINDALOO PASTE Ⓥ

This recipe is called "Goa ka vindaloo masala" in Hindi

Yield: Approximately 1 cup

Useful In making hot and tangy spicy dishes.

Ingredients:

- ¼ cup distilled white vinegar
- ½ cup Goan Vindaloo Powder (store-bought)
- 1 large onion, crudely chopped
- 2 teaspoons salt, or to taste
- 3 tablespoons peanut oil
- 3 to 4 dried red chile peppers, such chile de arbol, broken
- 30 to 40 fresh curry leaves
- 5 to 7 large cloves fresh garlic, peeled
- 8 to 10 quarter-size slices of peeled fresh ginger

Directions:

1. Immerse the red chile peppers in the vinegar, one to two hours. In the meantime, ready the vindaloo powder. Using a food processor, combine and pulse the red chile peppers, plus the vinegar, ginger, garlic, onion, curry leaves, and salt until a smooth paste is achieved. Stir in the vindaloo masala and process once more.
2. Heat the oil in a big non-stick wok or saucepan using moderate to high heat and stir-fry the paste, using moderate to high heat the first two to three minutes, and then over moderate heat until rich brown, approximately eight to ten minutes. Allow to cool, then store in an airtight vessel about thirty days in the fridge or six months in the freezer.

GUJARATI GREEN PASTE Ⓥ

This recipe is called "Gujerati hara masala" in Hindi

Yield: Approximately 1½ cups

A very hot and spicy paste from west India.

Ingredients:

- ¼ cup vegetable oil
- 4 to 6 ounces fresh green chile peppers, such as serrano, crudely chopped
- 6 ounces fresh garlic cloves, peeled
- 8 ounces fresh ginger, peeled and cut crosswise into thin round slices

Directions:

1. Using a food processor or a blender, combine and pulse all of the ingredients until high smoothness is achieved.
2. Move to an airtight vessel and place in your fridge for a maximum of 1 month, or freeze for no more than six months.

HYDERABADI GINGER-GARLIC PASTE Ⓥ

This recipe is called "Hyderabadi pissa adrak-lussan" in Hindi

Yield: Approximately 1½ cups

A Hyderabadi twist on a classic.

Ingredients:

- ¼ pound fresh garlic cloves, peeled
- ¾ pound fresh ginger, peeled and cut crosswise into thin round slices
- 1 to 3 tablespoons water

Directions:

1. You will a blander for this as a food processor just won't cut it. Mix together and pulse the ginger and garlic until the desired smoothness is achieved, pouring in water as required for blending.
2. Move to an airtight vessel and place in your fridge for a maximum of ten days or freeze for no more than six months.

KERALA FRIED ONION PASTE Ⓥ

This recipe is called "Kerala ka talae pyaz ka masala" in Hindi

Yield: Approximately 2 cups

A delicious paste with a hint of coconut.

Ingredients:

- ½ cup peanut oil
- 1 cup Coconut Milk (Homemade or store-bought)
- 15 to 20 fresh curry leaves
- 2 large onions, crudely chopped
- 5 large cloves fresh garlic, peeled
- 5 to 8 dried red chile peppers, such as chile de arbol, broken
- 6 to 8 quarter-size slices of peeled fresh ginger

Directions:

1. Heat the oil in a big non-stick saucepan using moderate to high heat and fry the red chile peppers and the onion until a golden colour is achieved, about three to four minutes. Put in the garlic, ginger, and curry leaves and fry until everything is well-browned, three to five minutes.
2. Cool, drain, and save the oil for future use. Then move to a blender or a food processor, put in the coconut milk and pulse until a smooth and thick paste is

achieved. Move to an airtight vessel and place in your fridge for a maximum of five days or freeze for no more than three months.

MINTY GREEN CURRY PASTE Ⓥ

This recipe is called "Pudinae vaala hara kari masala" in Hindi

Yield: Approximately 1 cup

Great for making minty curries.

Ingredients:

- ¼ cup peanut oil
- ½ cup crudely chopped fresh mint leaves
- 1 cup crudely chopped fresh cilantro, including soft stems
- 1 tablespoon fresh lime juice
- 1 teaspoon salt, or to taste
- 1 to 3 fresh green chile peppers, such as serrano, stemmed
- 1½ teaspoons garam masala
- 4 to 5 large cloves fresh garlic, peeled
- 5 to 6 scallions, crudely chopped with greens
- 6 quarter-size slices of peeled fresh ginger

Directions:

1. Using a food processor, combine and pulse the garlic, ginger, chile peppers, and scallions until minced. Put in the cilantro, mint, and lime juice and process until a smooth paste is achieved. Move to a container and stir in the garam masala and salt.
2. Heat the oil in a big non-stick wok or saucepan using moderate to high heat, put in the green paste and cook, stirring over moderate heat for the first two to three minutes and then using moderate to low heat until thoroughly browned, approximately ten to twelve minutes. Allow to cool, then store in an airtight vessel for approximately thirty days in the fridge or six months in the freezer.

MUGHLAI CURRY PASTE WITH NUTS

This recipe is called "Korma ka geela masala" in Hindi

Yield: Approximately 1 cup

Who doesn't live cream and nuts?

Ingredients:

- *2 tablespoons* Basic Ginger-Garlic Paste
- *½ cup* Fragrant Masala with Nuts
- ¼ cup heavy cream
- ½ cup non-fat plain yogurt
- 2 tablespoons melted ghee or vegetable oil

Directions:

1. Ready the paste and then the masala. Heat the ghee in a big non-stick saucepan using moderate to high heat, put in the ginger-garlic paste and korma masala and cook, stirring, until a mild brown colour is achieved.
2. In a container, whip together the cream and yogurt using a whisk or an electric beater, then add it to the saucepan in a thin stream, stirring continuously to stop curdling, until it is thoroughly blended with the paste. Allow to cool, then store in an airtight vessel in the fridge seven to ten days or three months in the freezer.

SPICY YELLOW CURRY PASTE Ⓥ

This recipe is called "Masaladar peela kari masala" in Hindi

Yield: Approximately 1 cup

A delicious combination of turmeric and red chile.

Ingredients:

- ¼ cup peanut oil
- 1 large onion, crudely chopped
- 1 tablespoon fresh lime juice
- 1 teaspoon cayenne pepper
- 1 teaspoon garam masala
- 1 teaspoon ground turmeric
- 1 teaspoon salt, or to taste
- 1 to 3 fresh green chile peppers, such as serrano, crudely chopped

- 10 quarter-size slices of peeled fresh ginger
- 4 to 5 large cloves fresh garlic, peeled

Directions:

1. Using a food processor, combine and pulse the ginger, garlic, chile peppers, onion, lime juice, turmeric, cayenne pepper, garam masala, and salt until a smooth paste is achieved.
2. Heat the oil in a big non-stick wok or sauce-pan, put in the paste, and cook, stirring using moderate to high heat the first two to three minutes and then using moderate to low heat until thoroughly browned, approximately ten to twelve minutes. Allow to cool, then store in an airtight vessel about thirty days in the fridge or six months in the freezer.

TAMARIND PASTE Ⓥ

This recipe is called "Imli ras" in Hindi

Yield: Approximately 1½ cups

You can easily buy this from a store, but make your own for better flavour.

Ingredients:

- 1½ cups warm water
- 6 ounces shelled fresh tamarind pods with seeds or 5 ounces tamarind pulp without seeds

Directions:

1. Immerse the shelled tamarind pods or pulp in 1 cup of the water, one to two hours to soften. Using your fingers, softly rub and mash the tamarind to loosen the pulp from the fibrous parts and to isolate the seeds.
2. Throw away the seeds and pass the softened pulp through a fine-mesh strainer or a food mill until a smooth paste is achieved. Move the fibrous remains to a container, mix the rest of the ½ cup water into the pulp and mash once more. Then pass through the sieve or food mill to extract more paste. Combine with the already extracted paste. Store in an airtight vessel about 1 week in the fridge or freeze measured amounts into ice cube trays and store the cubes in zip closure bags up to six months in the freezer.

CHUTNEY

Chutneys are basically spicy Indian sauces. They go great with not only Indian food, but also western food! Next time you're enjoying a steak, try it with some chutney on the side!

Indian chutneys can be broadly classified into two categories: fresh and preserved. In the fresh, perishable category we find the tangy purées of fresh herbs, spices, fruits, and yogurt. These chutneys stay fresh for about ten days in a fridge. If the chutney doesn't contain yogurt, if is safe to freeze. The fresh purées keep well in a freezer too. To freeze, pour the chutneys in serving-size containers or in ice-cube trays. Once they freeze, move to plastic zip-closure bags and freeze for no more than six months. Thaw at room temperature, or if you are in a rush, using a microwave.

The story with the non-perishable chutneys is a little different. These can be stores safely even at room temperature for long periods of time.

Ⓥ= Vegan Ⓟ= Quick Pressure Cooker Recipe

GREEN CHUTNEYS

BASIC GREEN CHUTNEY Ⓥ

This recipe is called "Hari chutni" in Hindi

Yield: Approximately 1½ cups

One of the most common chutneys you will see in India. Can be enjoyed with pretty much everything, and tastes absolutely amazing!

Ingredients:

- ½ teaspoon freshly ground black pepper, or to taste

- 1 cup fresh mint leaves, trimmed
- 1 teaspoon salt, or to taste
- 1 teaspoon sugar
- 2 to 3 cups crudely chopped fresh cilantro, including soft stems
- 2 to 5 fresh green chile peppers, such as serrano, stemmed
- 3 to 4 tablespoons fresh lime or lemon juice
- 6 to 8 scallions, just the green parts, crudely chopped

Directions:

1. Using a food processor or blender, combine and pulse the green chile peppers and scallion greens until minced. Put in the mint and cilantro to the work container and process, stopping intermittently to scrub the inner walls using a spatula, until puréed. While processing, trickle the lime juice through the feeder tube into the work container and pulse the chutney until the desired smoothness is achieved.
2. Put in the sugar, salt, and pepper and process once more. Tweak the seasonings to your taste. Move to a container and serve instantly, place in your fridge for approximately ten days, or freeze for no more than six months.

CILANTRO-LIME CHUTNEY Ⓥ

This recipe is called "Dhania chutni" in Hindi

Yield: Approximately 2 cups

A delicious chutney popular in all of India!

Ingredients:

- ½ cup fresh mint leaves
- ½ teaspoon cumin seeds, dry-roasted and crudely ground (See the Dry Roasting section in Introduction)
- 1 small green bell pepper, crudely chopped
- 1 teaspoon Chaat Masala (Homemade or store-bought)
- 1 teaspoon salt, or to taste
- 1 teaspoon sugar
- 2 to 3 tablespoons fresh lime or lemon juice

- 3 cups firmly packed, crudely chopped fresh cilantro, including soft stems
- 3 to 5 fresh green chile peppers, such as serrano, stemmed
- 4 quarter-size slices peeled fresh ginger
- 5 to 6 scallions, green parts only, crudely chopped

Directions:

1. Ready the cumin seeds and the chaat masala. Next, Using a food processor or a blender, blend together the green chile peppers, ginger, bell pepper, and scallion greens until minced. Put in the cilantro and mint to the work container and process, scraping the sides using a spatula a few times, until puréed. While processing, trickle the lime juice through the feeder tube into the work container and process to make a smooth chutney.
2. Put in the chaat masala, sugar, and salt and process once more. Tweak the seasonings to your taste. Move to a container and lightly stir in the cumin with some of it visible as a decoration. Serve instantly, place in your fridge for approximately ten days, or freeze for no more than six months.

MINT CHUTNEY Ⓥ

This recipe is called "Pudina-anardana chutni" in Hindi

Yield: Approximately 1½ cups

This chutney is a breath of freshness. Easily one of the favourite chutneys in India.

Ingredients:

- ½ teaspoon freshly ground black pepper
- 1 cup crudely chopped fresh cilantro, including soft stems
- 1 small red onion, crudely chopped
- 1 tablespoon fresh lemon juice
- 1 teaspoon salt, or to taste
- 1 teaspoon sugar
- 2 cups fresh mint leaves
- 2 teaspoons ground dried pomegranate seeds
- 2 to 4 tablespoons water
- 3 to 5 crudely chopped fresh green chile peppers, such as serrano, stemmed

Directions:

1. Add the onion, chile peppers, lemon juice, and 2 tablespoons of water to a blender and pulse until the desired smoothness is achieved. Put in the mint and cilantro in 2 batches, putting in more once the first batch becomes smooth, and pulse until thoroughly smooth. Put in the rest of the 2 tablespoons of the water, if required.
2. Put in the pomegranate seeds, pepper, sugar, and salt and blend once more. Tweak the seasonings to your taste. Move to a container and serve instantly, place in your fridge for approximately ten days, or freeze for no more than six months.

MINT-GARLIC CHUTNEY Ⓥ

This recipe is called "Pudina, lussan, moong-phalli aur imli ki chutni" in Hindi

Yield: Approximately 1½ cups

This chutney has a strong flavour, and goes great with fried snacks!

Ingredients:

- ⅛ teaspoon ground asafoetida
- ½ cup roasted peanuts, red skins removed
- 1 tablespoon peanut oil
- 1 teaspoon black mustard seeds
- 1 teaspoon salt, or to taste
- 1 teaspoon sugar
- 10 large cloves fresh garlic, peeled
- 2 cups packed fresh mint leaves
- 2 to 3 tablespoons <u>Tamarind Paste</u>
- 4 to 6 fresh green chile peppers, such as serrano, stemmed
- 5 to 6 fresh curry leaves

Directions:

1. Ready the tamarind paste. Next, Using a food processor or a blender, combine and pulse the peanuts, garlic, chile peppers, and mint until minced. Put in the

tamarind paste, sugar, and salt and process once more until a smooth purée is achieved. Put in a spoonful or 2 of water if required for blending. Tweak the seasonings to your taste. Move to a serving container.
2. Heat the oil in a big non-stick wok or saucepan using moderate to high heat and Put in the mustard seeds; they should splutter upon contact with the hot oil, so reduce the heat and cover the pan until the spluttering diminishes. Put in the curry leaves and asafoetida, stir for approximately half a minute, move to the chutney and stir mildly to combine, with parts of it visible as a decoration. Move to a container and serve instantly, place in your fridge for approximately ten days, or freeze for no more than six months.

SCALLION-GINGER CHUTNEY

This recipe is called "Harae pyaz aur adrak ki chutni" in Hindi

Yield: Approximately 1½ cups

This chutney has an intense hot flavour.

Ingredients:

- 1 (2½-inch) piece fresh ginger, peeled and cut into thin quarter-size rounds
- 1 cup fresh mint or cilantro leaves
- 1 teaspoon salt, or to taste
- 1 teaspoon sugar
- 12 to 15 young scallions, with green parts included, crudely chopped
- 2 to 3 tablespoons fresh lime or lemon juice
- 2 to 3 tablespoons non-fat plain yogurt
- 2 to 4 fresh green chile peppers, such as serrano, stemmed

Directions:

1. Put the chile peppers, ginger, scallion greens, lemon juice, and yogurt into a food processor or a blender and process until minced.
2. Put in the sugar, salt, and mint or cilantro leaves, and process to a smooth purée. Tweak the seasonings to your taste. Move to a container and serve instantly, place in your fridge for approximately ten days, or freeze for no more than six months.

SOUTH INDIAN CILANTRO CHUTNEY (V)

This recipe is called "Kothmir ki chutni" in Hindi

Yield: Approximately 1½ cups

A smooth South Indian chutney with an intense flavor.

Ingredients:

- ⅛ teaspoon ground asafoetida
- ¼ cup <u>Tamarind Paste</u>, or to taste
- 1 tablespoon dried white urad beans (dhulli urad dal), sorted
- 1 tablespoon peanut oil
- 1 teaspoon salt, or to taste
- 2 teaspoons black mustard seeds
- 3 cups firmly packed, crudely chopped fresh cilantro, including soft stems
- 4 to 6 dried red chile peppers, such as chile de arbol, crudely broken

Directions:

1. Ready the tamarind paste. Next, heat the oil in a small-sized non-stick saucepan over moderate heat and Put in the mustard seeds, red chile peppers, dal, and asafoetida. Cook, swaying the pan until the dal is golden, approximately one minute. Allow to cool and move to a blender and blend until as fine as possible.
2. Put in the tamarind paste and then Put in the cilantro in 2 or 3 batches, putting in more once the first batch becomes smooth. Add 2 to 3 tablespoons water, if required. Stir in the salt. Tweak the seasonings to your taste. Move to a container and serve instantly, place in your fridge for approximately ten days, or freeze for no more than six months.

COCONUT CHUTNEYS

FRESH COCONUT CHUTNEY WITH CILANTRO

This recipe is called "Nariyal aur dhania chutni" in Hindi

Yield: Approximately 2½ cups

Ingredients:

- ⅛ teaspoon ground asafoetida
- 1 cup crudely chopped fresh cilantro, including soft stems
- 1 cup plain yogurt, non-fat or any kind, whisked until the desired smoothness is achieved
- 1 fresh coconut
- 1 tablespoon coconut or peanut oil
- 1 teaspoon black mustard seeds
- 1 teaspoon salt, or to taste
- 2 tablespoons minced fresh curry leaves
- 2 to 3 tablespoons <u>South Indian Sambar Powder</u> (Homemade or store-bought)
- 3 quarter-size slices of peeled fresh ginger
- 3 tablespoons fresh lemon juice
- 3 to 5 fresh green chile peppers, such as serrano, stemmed

Directions:

1. Ready the sambar powder. Next, shell the coconut. Next, using a vegetable peeler, peel the brown skin off the flesh and discard. Crudely cut the coconut meat into ½- to 1-inch pieces. Using a food processor or a blender, combine and pulse the coconut, green chile peppers, and ginger until minced.
2. Put in the lemon juice, yogurt, and cilantro and process, scraping the sides of the work container a few times using a spatula until thoroughly smooth. Put in the salt and sambar powder and process once more. Tweak the seasonings to your taste, then move to a serving container.
3. Heat the oil in a small-sized non-stick saucepan using moderate to high heat and Put in the mustard seeds, curry leaves, and asafoetida; they should splutter upon contact with the hot oil, so reduce the heat and cover the pan until the spluttering diminishes. Swiftly add to the chutney and stir mildly with parts of it

visible as a decoration. Move to a container and serve instantly, place in your fridge for approximately ten days, or freeze for no more than six months.

MINTY COCONUT-TAMARIND CHUTNEY

(V)

This recipe is called "Nariyal aur Imli ki chutni" in Hindi

Yield: Approximately 1½ cups

Ingredients:

- ¼ cup fresh mint leaves
- ¼ cup Tamarind Paste
- ½ cup crudely chopped fresh cilantro, including soft stems
- 1 fresh coconut
- 1 teaspoon crudely ground dry-roasted cumin seeds (See the dry-roasting section in Introduction)
- 1 teaspoon salt, or to taste
- 2 large cloves fresh garlic, peeled
- 3 to 5 fresh green chile peppers, such as serrano, stemmed
- 6 to 8 quarter-size slices peeled fresh ginger

Directions:

1. Prepare cumin and tamarind paste. Next, shell the coconut. Using a vegetable peeler, peel the brown skin off the meat and discard. Crudely cut the coconut meat into ½- to 1-inch pieces. Using a food processor a blender, combine and pulse the coconut, ginger, green chile peppers, and garlic until minced.
2. Put in the cilantro, mint, tamarind, and salt and process, scraping the sides of the work container a few times using a spatula, until the desired smoothness is achieved. Tweak the seasonings to your taste, then move to a serving container. Garnish with the cumin and serve instantly, place in your fridge for approximately ten days, or freeze for no more than six months.

ROASTED COCONUT CHUTNEY Ⓥ

This recipe is called "Bhunae nariyal ki chutni" in Hindi

Yield: Approximately 1½ cups

Ingredients:

- ½ teaspoon fenugreek seeds
- 1 cup shredded or grated unsweetened dried coconut
- 1 scant pinch ground asafoetida
- 1 tablespoon coconut or peanut oil
- 1 tablespoon coriander seeds
- 1 tablespoon dried white split urad beans (dhulli urad dal), sorted
- 1 tablespoon dried yellow split chickpea (channa dal), sorted
- 1 teaspoon black mustard seeds
- 1 teaspoon cumin seeds
- 2 large cloves fresh garlic, crudely chopped
- 2 to 3 tablespoons <u>Tamarind Paste</u>
- 5 to 7 fresh curry leaves
- 7 dried red chile peppers, such as chile de arbol, 5 broken and 2 with stems

Directions:

1. Ready the tamarind paste. Next, preheat the oven to 250°F. Spread the coconut on a baking tray and roast until a golden colour is achieved, 20 to 30 minutes (depending on the moisture content).
2. In a small-sized non-stick saucepan, dry-roast together the broken red chile peppers, urad and channa dals, garlic, coriander, cumin, and fenugreek over moderate heat until seems slightly darker, approximately two minutes. Allow to cool, then grind using a spice or coffee grinder, in two batches if necessary, until a fine powder is achieved. Remove spices to a container. In the same grinder, grind the coconut, in two batches if necessary, to make it as fine as possible. Mix with the spices.
3. Heat the oil in a moderate-sized non-stick wok or saucepan using moderate to high heat and Put in the whole red chile peppers and mustard seeds; they should splutter upon contact with the hot oil, so reduce the heat and cover the pan until the spluttering diminishes. Put in the asafoetida and curry leaves, then stir in the coconut-spice mixture. Put in the tamarind paste and the salt, and stir over

moderate heat until well mixed. Move to a container and serve instantly, place in your fridge for approximately ten days, or freeze for no more than six months.

SEMOLINA-COCONUT CHUTNEY

This recipe is called "Sooji-kopra chutni" in Hindi

Yield: Approximately 1½ cups

Ingredients:

- ⅛ teaspoon ground asafoetida
- ⅓ cup fine-grain semolina
- ½ cup finely chopped fresh cilantro, including soft stems
- 1 cup non-fat plain yogurt
- 1 fresh green chile pepper, such as serrano, stemmed
- 1 tablespoon shredded or grated unsweetened dried coconut
- 1 teaspoon peanut oil
- 1 teaspoon salt, or to taste
- 15 to 20 fresh curry leaves
- 3 quarter-size slices of peeled fresh ginger

Directions:

1. Put the semolina and oil in a small-sized non-stick wok or saucepan and roast, stirring and swaying the pan using moderate to low heat, until the semolina is golden, approximately five minutes. Put in the coconut and asafoetida and cook, stirring, another two minutes.
2. Using a blender, mix together and pulse the yogurt, curry leaves, ginger, green chile pepper, and salt until the desired smoothness is achieved. Put in the roasted semolina and coconut mixture, and blend again until the desired smoothness is achieved. Allow to rest for approximately half an hour so the semolina can absorb the yogurt and expand. Move to a serving dish and refrigerate at least two hours. Stir in the cilantro and serve chilled. This chutney stays fresh in the fridge for approximately seven days. Do not freeze.

SHREDDED COCONUT CHUTNEY Ⓥ

This recipe is called "Kopra chutni" in Hindi

Yield: Approximately 1½ cups

Ingredients:

- ¼ to ⅓ cup water
- ½ cup crudely chopped fresh cilantro, including soft stems
- ½ teaspoon salt, or to taste
- ¾ cup fresh mint leaves
- 1¼ cups shredded or grated unsweetened dried coconut
- 2 fresh green chile peppers, such as serrano, stemmed
- 3 large cloves fresh garlic, peeled
- 3 to 4 tablespoons <u>Tamarind Paste</u>

Directions:

1. Ready the tamarind paste. Next, place the coconut in a medium size non-stick skillet and roast, stirring and swaying the pan over moderate heat until a golden colour is achieved, approximately two to three minutes.
2. Put all the rest of the ingredients using a blender or a food processor and process until a smooth purée is achieved. Stir in the roasted coconut and process once more until the desired smoothness is achieved. Move to a container and serve. This chutney stays fresh in the fridge for approximately ten days, or in the freezer about six months.

GARLIC AND CHILE PEPPER CHUTNEYS

GARLIC AND FRESH RED CHILE PEPPER CHUTNEY Ⓥ

This recipe is called "Lussan aur laal mirch ki chutni" in Hindi

Yield: Approximately 1½ cups

Ingredients:

- ¼ cup fresh lime juice, or to taste
- 1 tablespoon ground paprika
- 1 teaspoon cayenne pepper
- 1½ tablespoons ajwain seeds, crudely ground
- 15 to 20 fresh green chile peppers, such as serranos, crudely chopped
- 2 tablespoons black peppercorns, dry-roasted and ground (See the Dry Roasting section in Introduction)
- 2 to 3 red bell peppers, chopped
- 2 to 3 teaspoons salt, or to taste
- 6 to 8 large cloves fresh garlic, peeled
- 6 to 8 quarter-size slices of peeled fresh ginger

Directions:

1. Ready the peppercorns. Then place the garlic, ginger, red chile peppers, bell peppers, and lime juice Using a food processor or a blender and process until the desired smoothness is achieved. Put in the paprika, ajwain, 1½ tablespoons pepper, and the salt and process once more until the desired smoothness is achieved.
2. Move to a serving container, garnish with the rest of the pepper, and serve. This chutney stays fresh in the fridge for approximately thirty days or in the freezer about six months.
3. **Variation:** Make a simpler garlic chutney by processing together 2 large peeled heads fresh garlic, 2 teaspoons ground cayenne pepper, 1 small tomato, 1 teaspoon ground cumin seeds, and 1 teaspoon salt until a smooth paste is achieved.

GREEN GARLIC AND NUTS CHUTNEY Ⓥ

This recipe is called "Harae lussan aur nuts ki chutni" in Hindi

Yield: Approximately 1½ cups

Ingredients:

- ⅛ teaspoon ground asafoetida
- ¼ cup fresh lime or lemon juice, or to taste
- ¼ teaspoon ground paprika
- ½ cup fresh mint leaves
- ½ teaspoon black mustard seeds
- ½ teaspoon cumin seeds
- ½ teaspoon freshly ground black pepper, or to taste
- ¾ cup shelled and crudely chopped mixed raw nuts, such as walnuts, almonds, cashews, and pine nuts
- 1 tablespoon vegetable oil
- 1 teaspoon sugar
- 1½ cups crudely chopped fresh cilantro, including soft stems
- 1½ teaspoons salt, or to taste
- 3 to 5 fresh green chile peppers, such as serrano, stemmed
- 5 to 7 green garlic shoots (with bulbs), bottom 3 to 4 inches only, thinly chopped

Directions:

1. Using a food processor or a blender, combine and pulse the nuts, green chile peppers and garlic until minced. Put in the cilantro and mint to the work container and process, stopping intermittently to scrub the inner walls using a spatula, until puréed. While processing, trickle the lime juice through the feeder tube into the work container and pulse the chutney until the desired smoothness is achieved. Put in the sugar, salt, and black pepper and process once more. Tweak the seasonings to your taste. Move to a container.
2. Heat the oil in a big non-stick wok or saucepan using moderate to high heat and Put in the cumin and mustard seeds; they should splatter upon contact with the hot oil, so reduce the heat and cover the pan and reduce the heat until the splattering diminishes. Mix in the asafoetida and paprika just to blend, then move the spice mixture to the chutney and stir mildly to combine, with parts of it

visible as a decoration. Move to a container and serve instantly, place in your fridge for approximately ten days, or freeze for no more than six months.

PEANUT AND GARLIC CHUTNEY Ⓥ

This recipe is called "Moong-phalli aur lassun ki chutni" in Hindi

Yield: Approximately 1½ cups

Ingredients:

- ¼ cup Tamarind Paste or lemon juice
- ½ cup dried shredded unsweetened coconut
- ½ teaspoon salt, or to taste
- 1 tablespoon peanut oil
- 1 teaspoon black mustard seeds
- 1¼ cups roasted unsalted peanuts, without red skin
- 2 large cloves fresh garlic, peeled
- 4 to 5 dried red chile peppers, such as chiles de arbol, broken
- 5 to 7 fresh curry leaves

Directions:

1. Ready the tamarind paste. Next, in a small skillet, dry-roast the red chile peppers until seems slightly darker. Put the peppers Using a food processor or a blender. Put in the peanuts and process until fine. Then Put in the coconut, garlic, tamarind (or lemon juice), and salt, and pulse until a smooth and thick paste is achieved, adding up to ¼ cup water, as needed.
2. Move to a serving container. Heat the oil in a small saucepan using moderate to high heat. Put in the mustard seeds and curry leaves; they should splutter upon contact with the hot oil, so cover the pan until the spluttering diminishes. Swiftly put in the spice mixture to the chutney and stir mildly to combine, with parts of it visible as a decoration. Move to a container and serve instantly, place in your fridge for approximately ten days, or freeze for no more than six months.

BEAN AND LEGUME CHUTNEYS

CLASSIC HYDERABADI GINGER-SESAME CHUTNEY Ⓥ

This recipe is called "Hyderabad ki adrak-til chutni" in Hindi

Yield: Approximately 1½ cups

Ingredients:

- ⅛ teaspoon ground asafoetida
- ¼ cup <u>Tamarind Paste</u>, or to taste
- 1 cup peeled and crudely chopped fresh ginger
- 1 large clove fresh garlic, peeled
- 1 tablespoon white sesame seeds
- 1 teaspoon black mustard seeds
- 1 teaspoon cumin seeds
- 1 teaspoon salt, or to taste
- 1 to 3 fresh green chile peppers, such as serrano, chopped with seeds
- 2 dried red chile peppers, such as chile de arbol, broken
- 2 tablespoons grated jaggery (gur)
- 2 teaspoons Indian sesame oil
- 8 to 10 fresh curry leaves

Directions:

1. Ready the tamarind paste. Next, heat the oil in a small-sized non-stick saucepan using moderate to low heat and cook the ginger, stirring, until a golden colour is achieved, approximately five minutes. Using a slotted spoon, remove the fried ginger to a blender jar, leaving the oil behind in the pan.
2. In the same oil, put in the garlic and the green and red chile peppers and cook, stirring, until a golden colour is achieved. Tilt the pan to gather the oil to one side and Put in the cumin and mustard seeds; they should splutter upon contact with

the hot oil, so reduce the heat and cover the pan until the spluttering diminishes. Swiftly put in the curry leaves, sesame seeds, and asafoetida.
3. Move to the blender jar, put in the jaggery, tamarind paste, and the salt, and process until crudely puréed. Put in a tablespoon or 2 of hot water, if required, for blending. Move to a container and serve instantly, place in your fridge for approximately ten days, or freeze for no more than six months.

ROASTED BLACK CHICKPEA CHUTNEY WITH PEANUTS Ⓥ

This recipe is called "Kaalae channae ki chutni" in Hindi

Yield: Approximately 1½ cups

Ingredients:

- ¼ teaspoon salt, or to taste
- ½ cup crudely chopped fresh cilantro, including soft stems
- ½ cup dry-roasted unsalted peanuts, red skin removed
- ½ cup roasted black chickpeas (bhunae channae)
- ½ teaspoon sugar
- 1 to 2 fresh green chile peppers, such as serrano, stemmed
- 1 to 2 tablespoons fresh lime or lemon juice

Directions:

1. Rub off the black outer coating from the chickpeas (it comes off easily). Using a spice or coffee grinder, mix together and grind the chickpeas and peanuts until the desired smoothness is achieved.
2. Using a food processor or a blender, combine and pulse the cilantro, chile peppers, and lime juice, and then Put in the ground dal, peanuts, sugar, and salt. Process until well mixed. Move to a container and serve instantly, place in your fridge for approximately ten days, or freeze for no more than six months.

ROASTED DAL AND FRESH GREEN CHILE PEPPER CHUTNEY Ⓥ

This recipe is called "Bhel-puri ki chutni" in Hindi

Yield: Approximately 1½ cups

Ingredients:

- ¾ cup dried yellow split chickpeas (channa dal), sorted and washed in 3 to 4 changes of water
- 1½ teaspoons salt, or to taste
- 2 cups crudely chopped fresh cilantro, including soft stems
- 20 to 25 fresh green chile peppers, such as serrano, stemmed
- 3 to 4 tablespoons fresh lemon or lime juice
- 4 large cloves fresh garlic, peeled

Directions:

1. Put the dal in a small-sized cast-iron or non-stick skillet and dry-roast using moderate heat, stirring and swaying the pan until a golden colour is achieved, approximately a minute or two. Allow to cool, then grind using a spice or coffee grinder till you get a fine powder.
2. Put the cilantro, green chile peppers, garlic, and lemon juice using a blender or a food processor and process until the desired smoothness is achieved. Put in the ground dal and the salt and process once again to mix. Move to a container and serve instantly, place in your fridge for approximately ten days, or freeze for no more than six months.

SESAME-PEANUT CHUTNEY Ⓥ

This recipe is called "Til aur moong-phalli ki chutni" in Hindi

Yield: Approximately 1 cup

Ingredients:

- ¼ cup hot water
- ¼ cup white sesame seeds
- ½ cup crudely chopped fresh cilantro, including soft stems
- ½ cup dry-roasted unsalted peanuts, red skins removed
- ½ cup Tamarind Paste
- 1 large clove fresh garlic, peeled
- 1 teaspoon salt, or to taste
- 1 to 3 fresh green chile peppers, such as serrano, stemmed

Directions:

1. Ready the tamarind paste. Next, in a small skillet, roast the sesame seeds over moderate heat, stirring and swaying the pan until a golden colour is achieved, approximately one minute. Move to a blender along with all the other ingredients and pulse until the desired smoothness is achieved.
2. Tweak the seasonings to your taste. Move to a container and serve instantly, place in your fridge for approximately ten days, or freeze for no more than six months.

YOGURT CHUTNEYS

YOGURT CHEESE CHUTNEY WITH MINCED GREENS

This recipe is called "Gaadhi dahi ki hari chutni" in Hindi

Yield: Approximately 1½ cups

Ingredients:

- ¼ cup minced fresh cilantro, including soft stems
- ¼ cup minced fresh mint leaves
- ¼ teaspoon ground paprika

- 1 (2-foot-square) piece of fine muslin or 4 layers of cheesecloth
- 1 fresh green chile pepper, such as serrano, minced with seeds
- 1 tablespoon peeled and minced fresh ginger
- 1 teaspoon Chaat Masala, or to taste (Homemade or store-bought)
- 1 teaspoon dry-roasted and crudely crushed cumin seeds (See the dry-roasting section in Introduction)
- 10 to 12 scallions, white parts only, minced
- 1½ cups non-fat plain yogurt
- 2 tablespoons fresh lemon juice

Directions:

1. Ready the cumin and the chaat masala. Next, place the yogurt in a colander or a fine-mesh strainer lined with muslin or 4 layers of cheesecloth set over a container. let drain about two hours in a fridge. Move to a serving container, then whisk with a fork until the desired smoothness is achieved.
2. Put in the scallion, cilantro, mint, ginger, green chile pepper, lemon juice, chaat masala, sugar, and half the cumin, and mix thoroughly. Tweak the seasonings to your taste. Garnish with the rest of the cumin seeds and the paprika, and serve instantly or place in your fridge for approximately seven days. Do not freeze.

YOGURT CHUTNEY WITH PURÉED GREENS

This recipe is called "Dahi ki hari chutni" in Hindi

Yield: Approximately 1½ cups

Ingredients:

- ½ teaspoon crudely ground black pepper
- 1 cup non-fat plain yogurt, whisked until the desired smoothness is achieved
- 1 teaspoon Chaat Masala, or to taste (Homemade or store-bought)
- 1 teaspoon salt, or to taste
- 1 to 3 fresh green chile peppers, such as serrano, stemmed
- 2 cups crudely chopped mixed fresh herbs in any proportion, such as cilantro, mint, parsley, dill, basil, or lemon basil

- 2 tablespoons fresh lime or lemon juice
- 4 quarter-size slices of peeled fresh ginger
- 5 to 6 scallions, crudely chopped
- Minced fresh greens of your choice (scallions, chile peppers, or herbs)

Directions:

1. Ready the chaat masala. Next, Using a food processor or a blender, combine and pulse the ginger, scallions, and green chile peppers until minced. Put in the fresh herbs and lime juice and process once more until the desired smoothness is achieved, scraping the sides of the work container using a spatula, as required. (If you need more liquid while processing, stir in some of the yogurt.) Put in the chaat masala, salt, and pepper, and process once more.
2. Put the yogurt in a serving container and Put in the puréed greens. Swirl lightly to combine, with parts of the greens visible as a decoration. Scatter the additional minced greens on top, and serve. This chutney stays fresh in the fridge for approximately seven days. Do not freeze.

YOGURT CHUTNEY WITH ROASTED DALS AND SPICES

This recipe is called "Dahi aur bhuni dal ki chutni" in Hindi

Yield: Approximately 1½ cups

Ingredients:

- ¼ cup grated fresh or frozen coconut
- ¼ teaspoon ground asafoetida
- ½ cup crudely chopped fresh cilantro, including soft stems
- 1 cup non-fat plain yogurt, whisked until the desired smoothness is achieved
- 1 tablespoon each, dried yellow split chickpeas (channa dal), split white urad beans (dhulli urad dal), yellow mung beans (dhulli mung dal), dry-roasted and ground (See the dry-roasting section in Introduction)
- 1 tablespoon vegetable oil
- 1 teaspoon black mustard seeds
- 1 teaspoon salt, or to taste

- 1 to 2 fresh green chile peppers, such as serrano, crudely chopped
- 15 to 20 fresh curry leaves
- 2 dried red chile peppers, such as chile de arbol, with stems, broken
- 2 tablespoons peeled and crudely chopped fresh ginger
- 2 teaspoons cumin seeds, dry-roasted and crudely ground (See the dry-roasting section in Introduction)

Directions:

1. Ready the dals and the cumin. Then heat the oil in a small-sized non-stick wok or saucepan using moderate to high heat and Put in the red chile peppers and mustard seeds; they should splutter upon contact with the hot oil, so reduce the heat and cover the pan until the spluttering diminishes.
2. Swiftly put in the asafoetida, curry leaves, green chile peppers, coconut, and ginger, and cook, stirring, until the coconut is golden, approximately five minutes. Put in the cilantro and stir another 5 minutes. Move to a blender or a food processor and process until a smooth paste is achieved.
3. Put the yogurt in a serving container, stir in the processed herb and coconut paste, then Put in the roasted dals, cumin (save some cumin for garnish), and the salt, and stir to mix thoroughly. Sprinkle the reserved cumin on top and serve. This chutney stays fresh in the fridge for approximately seven days. Do not freeze.

YOGURT-ALMOND CHUTNEY

This recipe is called "Dahi-badaam ki chutni" in Hindi

Yield: Approximately 1½ cups

Ingredients:

- ¼ cup minced fresh cilantro, including soft stems
- ½ cup shelled and crudely ground raw almonds
- 1 cup non-fat plain yogurt, whisked until the desired smoothness is achieved
- 1 fresh green chile pepper, such as serrano, minced with seeds
- 1 tablespoon fresh lemon juice
- 1 tablespoon peeled and minced fresh ginger
- 1 teaspoon <u>Chaat Masala</u> (Homemade or store-bought)

- 1 teaspoon salt, or to taste
- Freshly ground black pepper, to taste

Directions:

1. In a serving container, combine all the ingredients except the chaat masala and chill at least 4 hours.
2. Before serving, ready the chaat masala then add it to the chutney and stir mildly to combine, with parts of it visible as a decoration. This chutney stays fresh about seven days in a fridge. Do not freeze.

PURÉED FRUIT CHUTNEYS

PURÉED FRESH MANGO-GINGER CHUTNEY Ⓥ

This recipe is called "Pakkae aam ki chutni" in Hindi

Yield: Approximately 1½ cups

Ingredients:

- ¼ cup finely chopped fresh cilantro, including soft stems
- ¼ cup fresh lime or lemon juice
- ½ teaspoon salt, or to taste
- 1 to 2 fresh green chile pepper, such as serrano, minced with seeds
- 2 tablespoons peeled and minced fresh ginger
- 3 large ripe mangoes (about ¾ pound each), washed and wiped dry
- Freshly ground black pepper

Directions:

1. Using a knife, peel the mango, then crudely cut the fruit around the center seed. Put the mango pieces in a big serving container and mash with a fork to make the fruit as smooth as possible.
2. Stir in all the rest of the ingredients. Garnish with black pepper and serve instantly, or place in your fridge for a maximum of seven days.

PURÉED GREEN MANGO CHUTNEY Ⓥ

This recipe is called "Harae aam ki chutni" in Hindi

Yield: Approximately 1½ cups

Ingredients:

- ⅛ teaspoon ground asafoetida
- ½ teaspoon crudely ground fenugreek seeds
- ½ teaspoon salt, or to taste
- 1 tablespoon peanut oil
- 1 teaspoon black mustard seeds
- 1 to 2 teaspoons sugar (not compulsory)
- 1 to 3 fresh green chile peppers, such as serrano, stemmed
- 15 to 20 fresh curry leaves
- 2 large unripe green mangoes (about ¾ pound each), washed and wiped dry
- 2 whole dried red chile peppers, such as chile de arbol
- 3 quarter-size slices peeled fresh ginger
- 4 scallions, crudely chopped

Directions:

1. Using a vegetable peeler, peel the mangoes, then cut the fruit around the center seed into ½- to 1-inch pieces. Put the mango pieces and the ginger, green chile peppers, scallions, curry leaves, and salt Using a food processor or a blender, and process until minced. Transfer to a serving container. Add some of the sugar if the chutney appears too tart.
2. Heat the oil in a small-sized non-stick saucepan using moderate to high heat and Put in the red chile peppers and mustard seeds; they should splutter upon contact with the hot oil, so reduce the heat and cover the pan until the spluttering diminishes. Swiftly put in the fenugreek seeds and asafoetida, stir for

about half a minute, then add this seasoning mixture to the chutney, with parts of it visible as a decoration. Move to a container and serve instantly, place in your fridge for approximately ten days, or freeze for no more than six months.

SOUTH INDIAN TOMATO CHUTNEY Ⓥ

This recipe is called "South ki tamatar chutni" in Hindi

Yield: Approximately 1½ cups

Ingredients:

- ¼ cup peanut oil
- ½ cup finely chopped red onion
- ½ teaspoon black peppercorns
- 1 (15-ounce) can tomato sauce
- 1 tablespoon coriander seeds
- 1 teaspoon black mustard seeds
- 1 teaspoon cayenne pepper, or to taste
- 1 teaspoon cumin seeds
- 1 teaspoon dried curry leaves
- 1 teaspoon dried white urad beans (dhulli urad dal), sorted
- 1 teaspoon dried yellow split chickpeas (channa dal), sorted
- 1 teaspoon salt, or to taste
- 1 teaspoon Tamarind Paste
- 2 large cloves fresh garlic, minced
- 2 to 3 whole dried red chile peppers, such as chile de arbol

Directions:

1. Ready the tamarind paste. Next, in a spice or a coffee grinder, mix together and grind coriander and cumin seeds, dals, and peppercorns until a fine powder is achieved.
2. Heat the oil in a small-sized non-stick saucepan over moderate heat and Put in the mustard seeds, curry leaves, and red chile peppers; they should splutter upon contact with the hot oil, so reduce the heat and cover the pan until the spluttering diminishes. Swiftly put in the garlic and onion, stir a few sec-onds,

then Put in the ground spice and dal mixture, cayenne pepper, and salt and cook, stirring, another two minutes.
3. Put in the tomato sauce and tamarind paste, cover the pan, reduce the heat to low, and cook, stirring intermittently, until the chutney is thick and fragrant and reduced to about 1 cup, approximately twenty minutes. Allow to cool, then serve instantly, place in your fridge for approximately sixty days or freeze about six months.

TART APPLE-GINGER CHUTNEY Ⓥ

This recipe is called "Saeb, adrak aur harae tamatar ki chutni" in Hindi

Yield: Approximately 2 cups

Ingredients:

- 1 tablespoon coriander seeds
- 1 tablespoon peanut oil
- 1 teaspoon black peppercorns, dry-roasted and crudely ground (See the Dry Roasting section in Introduction)
- 1 teaspoon salt, or to taste
- 1 teaspoon sugar
- 2 fresh green chile peppers, such as serrano, stemmed
- 2 large tart green apples, such as Granny Smith or pippin, cored and crudely chopped
- 2 small green tomatoes, crudely chopped
- 6 to 8 quarter-size slices of peeled fresh ginger
- Fresh cilantro sprigs

Directions:

1. Ready the peppercorns. Then heat the oil in a small saucepan using moderate to high heat and Put in the coriander seeds; they should sizzle upon contact with the hot oil. Swiftly put in the rest of the ingredients and cook, stirring, approximately five minutes.
2. Move to a food processor or a blender and process to make a coarse purée. Move to a container, garnish with cilantro sprigs, and serve. This chutney stays

fresh in the fridge for approximately ten days, and in the freezer about six months.

PRESERVED CHUTNEYS

CRANBERRY CHUTNEY PRESERVE Ⓥ

This recipe is called "Karonda chutni" in Hindi

Yield: Approximately 4 cups

Ingredients:

- 1 tablespoon ground ginger
- 1 tablespoon vegetable oil
- 10 to 12 whole cloves
- 1½ teaspoons salt, or to taste
- 2 (12-ounce) packages fresh cranberries, washed
- 2 (1-inch) sticks cinnamon
- 2 tablespoons Bengali 5-Spices (Panch-Phoran), crudely ground
- 2 tablespoons peeled and minced fresh ginger
- 4 cups sugar
- 4 cups water
- 5 to 7 tablespoons distilled white vinegar
- 8 to 10 black cardamom pods, crushed lightly to break the skin

Directions:

1. Ready the 5-spices. Next, heat the oil in a big non-reactive wok or saucepan using moderate to high heat and cook the cinnamon, cardamom pods, and cloves, stirring, approximately half a minute.
2. Put in the fresh ginger and panch-phoran and cook, stirring, approximately one minute. Put in the cranberries, sugar, water, ground ginger, and salt, and bring to

a boil using high heat. Cover and cook, stirring intermittently, until slightly thickened, approximately 7 minutes.
3. Reduce the heat to medium, uncover the pan, put in the vinegar, and cook until the chutney is quite thick, approximately ten minutes. (Do not make the chutney very thick; it will thicken as it cools.) Move to a container, allow to cool down, and serve at room temperature, or refrigerate at least two hours and serve chilled. This chutney stays fresh in the fridge for approximately three months, or in the freezer about 1 year.

FRAGRANT MANGO CHUTNEY PRESERVE
(V)

This recipe is called "Aam ki chutni" in Hindi

Yield: Approximately 4 cups

Ingredients:

- ¾ cup distilled white vinegar
- 1 tablespoon black peppercorns
- 1 tablespoon fennel seeds
- 1 tablespoon fenugreek seeds
- 1 tablespoon salt, or to taste
- 1 tablespoon whole cloves
- 10 to 12 black cardamom pods, crushed lightly to break the skin
- 10 to 12 green cardamom pods, crushed lightly to break the skin
- 1½ teaspoons kalonji seeds
- 2 (3-inch) sticks cinnamon, broken
- 4 cups sugar
- 4 large unripe green mangoes, (about ¾ pound each), washed and wiped dry

Directions:

1. Using a vegetable peeler, peel the mangoes, then cut the fruit around the center seed into thin 1½- to 2-inch long pieces. Put all the spices in a large, heavy, non-reactive saucepan and roast using moderate to high heat, stirring and swaying the pan, until heated through, approximately one minute.

2. Put in the mangoes, sugar, and salt, and bring to a boil, stirring continuously using moderate to high heat until the sugar melts and comes to a boil. Boil 1 minute, then reduce the heat to medium-low, cover the pan and cook, stirring intermittently, approximately ten minutes.
3. Uncover the pan, put in the vinegar, and cook, stirring intermittently, until the sugar caramelizes and takes on a rich honey-like color and consistency, approximately twenty minutes. (Do not make the chutney very thick; it will thicken as it cools.)
4. Allow to cool completely, then put it in sterile jars. This chutney does not need to be refrigerated. It stays fresh about six months at room temperature. The color deepens over time, but that does not affect the taste.

RED TOMATO CHUTNEY PRESERVE Ⓥ

This recipe is called "Tamatar-til ki chutni" in Hindi

Yield: Approximately 2 cups

Ingredients:

- ⅛ teaspoon ground asafoetida
- ¼ teaspoon ground turmeric
- 1 cup finely chopped onion
- 1 tablespoon black mustard seeds
- 1 tablespoon dried split pigeon peas (toor dal), sorted
- 1 tablespoon dried yellow split chickpeas (channa dal), sorted
- 1 tablespoon minced fresh garlic cloves
- 1 tablespoon sesame seeds, dry-roasted (See the dry-roasting section in Introduction)
- 1 teaspoon salt, or to taste
- 1 to 3 fresh green chile peppers, such as serrano, minced with seeds
- 2 large tomatoes, finely chopped
- 2 tablespoons distilled white vinegar
- 2 tablespoons minced fresh curry leaves
- 2 tablespoons peanut oil
- 2 tablespoons peeled and minced fresh ginger

Directions:

1. Ready the sesame seeds. Next, heat the oil in a medium wok or saucepan using moderate to high heat and Put in the mustard seeds; they should splutter upon contact with the hot oil, so reduce the heat and cover the pan until the spluttering diminishes. Put in the curry leaves and both the dals, and stir until the dals are golden, approximately half a minute. Put in the onion and cook, stirring, until a golden colour is achieved, approximately three minutes. Put in the ginger, garlic, and green chile peppers, stir 1 minute, then stir in the turmeric, salt, and asafoetida.
2. Put in the tomatoes and vinegar and cook until most of the fluids vaporize and the chutney is semi-thick, approximately eight to ten minutes. (It will continue to thicken as it cools.) Move to a serving dish, garnish with the sesame seeds, and serve hot or cold, or store in an airtight vessel in the refrigerator, approximately 1 year.

SPICY APPLE-GINGER CHUTNEY PRESERVE Ⓥ

This recipe is called "Saeb-adrak ki chutni" in Hindi

Yield: Approximately 4 cups

Ingredients:

- ¼ cup distilled white vinegar
- 10 whole cloves
- 1½ tablespoons salt
- 2 cups sugar
- 2 medium onions, cut in half along the length and thinly chopped
- 2 pounds tart apples, such as Pippin or Granny Smith, peeled and cut in ½-inch pieces
- 2 tablespoons <u>Basic Ginger-Garlic Paste</u> (Homemade or store-bought)
- 2 tablespoons fennel seeds
- 2 teaspoons crudely ground fenugreek seeds
- 2 teaspoons kalonji seeds
- 2 to 3 teaspoons cayenne pepper

- 20 to 25 dried red chile peppers, such as chile de arbol, with stems
- 3 tablespoons vegetable oil
- 4 (1-inch) sticks cinnamon
- 5 to 6 (1-inch) pieces peeled fresh ginger, cut in half along the length and thinly chopped
- 6 fresh garlic cloves, cut in half along the length and thinly chopped
- 6 to 8 black cardamom pods, crushed lightly to break the skin

Directions:

1. Ready the ginger-garlic paste. Next, heat the oil in a big non-stick wok or saucepan using moderate to high heat and cook the red chile peppers, cinnamon, cardamom pods, and cloves, stirring, approximately one minute. Put in the fennel and kalonji seeds, and stir for approximately half a minute, then Put in the onion, ginger, and garlic and cook, stirring until a golden colour is achieved, approximately ten minutes.
2. Put in the fenugreek seeds and cayenne pepper and stir 1 minute. Then Put in the apples, sugar, ginger-garlic paste, and salt, and cook over moderate heat, stirring, until the sugar melts, approximately three minutes. Increase the heat to medium-high and cook until the sugar caramelizes into a rich golden color, the apples are soft, and the chutney is thick, approximately fifteen minutes.
3. Put in the vinegar and boil using high heat approximately two minutes, or until the chutney thickens once more. (Do not make the chutney very thick; it will thicken as it cools.) Allow to cool completely and put in sterile jars. This chutney does not need to be refrigerated. It stays fresh about six months at room temperature. The color deepens over time, but that does not affect the taste.

SPICY APRICOT CHUTNEY PRESERVE Ⓥ

This recipe is called "Aadu ki chutni" in Hindi

Yield: Approximately 4 cups

Ingredients:

- ¼ cup Basic Ginger-Garlic Paste (Homemade or store-bought)
- ¼ to ⅓ cup distilled white vinegar
- ¾ teaspoon ground fenugreek seeds

- 1 tablespoon ground fennel seeds
- 1 teaspoon kalonji seeds
- 1½ cups sugar
- 2 pounds fresh unripe apricots, pitted and cut into wedges
- 2 tablespoons salt, or to taste
- 3 (1-inch) sticks cinnamon
- 3 small onions, cut in half along the length and thinly chopped
- 3 tablespoons vegetable oil
- 5 to 7 fresh green chile peppers, such as serrano, minced with seeds
- 6 to 8 black cardamom pods, crushed lightly to break the skin
- 8 whole cloves

Directions:

1. Ready the ginger-garlic paste. Next, heat the oil in a big non-stick wok or saucepan using moderate to high heat and cook the cinnamon, cardamom pods, and cloves, stirring, approximately one minute. Put in the onions and cook, stirring, until a golden colour is achieved, approximately 7 minutes. Put in the kalonji, fenugreek, and fennel seeds, and then stir in the ginger-garlic paste and green chile peppers and sauté approximately two minutes.
2. Put in the apricots, sugar, and salt and cook, stir-ring, over moderate heat until the sugar melts, approximately three minutes. Increase the heat to medium-high and cook until the sugar caramelizes into a rich golden color, the apricots are soft, and the chutney is thick, approximately fifteen minutes.
3. Put in the vinegar, and boil using high heat approximately two minutes, or until the chutney thickens once more. (Do not make the chutney very thick; it will thicken as it cools.) Allow to cool completely, and put in sterile jars. This chutney does not need to be refrigerated. It stays fresh about six months at room temperature. The color deepens over time, but that does not affect the taste.

TOMATO CHUTNEY PRESERVE Ⓥ

This recipe is called "Tamatar, kaaju aur kishmish ki chutni" in Hindi

Yield: Approximately 2 cups

Ingredients:

- ½ cup crudely chopped raw cashews
- ½ cup distilled white vinegar
- ½ cup golden raisins
- ½ teaspoon crudely crushed fenugreek seeds
- ½ teaspoon cayenne pepper
- 1 tablespoon salt, or to taste
- 1 tablespoon vegetable oil
- 1 teaspoon fennel seeds
- 1 teaspoon ground paprika
- 2 cups sugar, or more to taste
- 2 large fresh garlic cloves, minced
- 2 tablespoons peeled and minced fresh ginger
- 2 to 4 fresh green chile peppers, minced with seeds
- 3 large tomatoes, finely chopped (about 1½ pounds)

Directions:

1. Heat the oil in a big non-reactive wok or saucepan over moderate heat and cook the ginger, garlic, green chile peppers, fennel seeds and fenugreek seeds, stirring, until a golden colour is achieved, approximately one minute. Put in the cashews and raisins and stir until the raisins expand, approximately one minute.
2. Put in the tomatoes, sugar, salt, paprika, and cayenne pepper and cook, using moderate to high heat for the first two to three minutes. Then cover the pan and cook, stirring intermittently, over moderate heat until the tomatoes are very soft, approximately ten minutes. Put in the vinegar, and simmer, uncovered, until semi-thick, approximately fifteen minutes. (It will continue to thicken as it cools.) Serve instantly or allow to cool down, then store in an airtight vessel in the refrigerator, approximately 1 year.

SONTH CHUTNEYS

These are delicious sweet and sour chutneys commonly seen in Indian restaurants.

MINTY SONTH CHUTNEY WITH MANGO

Ⓥ

This recipe is called "Pudina sonth" in Hindi

Yield: Approximately 4 cups

Ingredients:

- ½ teaspoon black salt
- ½ teaspoon ground ginger
- 1 cup crudely grated or crushed jaggery, or 1¼ cup dark brown sugar
- 1 cup mango or tamarind powder, sifted to remove any lumps
- 1 teaspoon ground paprika
- 1 to 3 fresh green chile peppers, such as serrano, stemmed
- 1½ tablespoons cumin seeds, dry-roasted and crudely ground (See the dry-roasting section in Introduction)
- 2 tablespoons <u>Chaat Masala</u> (Homemade or store-bought)
- 2 teaspoon salt, or to taste
- 20 to 25 large fresh mint leaves
- 3 to 4 cups water
- 8 quarter-size slices of peeled fresh ginger

Directions:

1. Ready the cumin seeds and chaat masala. Next, in a blender, mix together and pulse the ginger, chile peppers, mint leaves with about ½ cup of the water until a smooth paste is achieved.
2. In a large non-reactive saucepan, combine the jaggery and 3 cups of the water (disregard any lumps; they will melt when heated) and bring to a boil, stirring intermittently, until all the lumps dissolve completely, about three to four minutes. Pass through a fine-mesh strainer to filter out any impurities. Put the jaggery back into the saucepan and Put in the ginger-mint mixture, mango or tamarind powder, chaat masala, paprika, ground ginger, cumin, salt, and black salt.
3. Bring to a boil using high heat. Reduce the heat to moderate to low, and simmer, stirring intermittently, approximately five minutes. The sauce should be like a semi-thick batter. Stir in up to 1 cup of water if the sauce becomes thick too

swiftly. Adjust seasoning, move to a container, then allow to cool down. Serve at room temperature. Or move to an airtight vessel and place in your fridge for approximately sixty days, or freeze about 1 year.

SONTH CHUTNEY WITH DRIED MANGO SLICES Ⓥ Ⓟ

This recipe is called "Amchur ki sonth" in Hindi

Yield: Approximately 4 cups

Ingredients:

- 1 (2-inch) piece dried ginger, crudely chopped
- 1 cup crudely grated or crushed jaggery, or 1¼ cups dark brown sugar
- 1 tablespoon Chaat Masala, or to taste (Homemade or store-bought)
- 1 tablespoon cumin seeds, dry-roasted and finely ground (See the dry-roasting section in Introduction)
- 1 teaspoon black salt
- 1 teaspoon ground paprika
- 2 teaspoons salt, or to taste
- 4 cups water
- 4 ounces dried raw mango slices
- 4 to 6 dried red chile peppers, such as chile de arbol, broken

Directions:

1. Ready the cumin seeds and chaat masala. Next, place everything (except 1 cup of the water) into your pressure cooker. Ensure that the lid is secure, and cook using high heat until the regulator shows that the pressure is high, then cook for approximately a minute more. Take the pot off the heat or turn off the heat and let the pressure release automatically, twelve to fifteen minutes. Cautiously take the lid off.
2. Pass everything through a food mill into a big container to extract a smooth sauce. Bring the reserved one cup of water to a boil in a small saucepan. Pour the boiling hot water over the fibrous residue in the food mill and collect the rest of the pulp. Mix the extra pulp into the sauce; it should be like a semi-thick batter.

Tweak the seasonings to your taste, move to a container and serve at room temperature, or move to an airtight vessel and place in your fridge for approximately sixty days, or freeze about 1 year.

SONTH CHUTNEY WITH FRESH AND DRIED FRUITS Ⓥ

This recipe is called "Fallon vaali sonth" in Hindi

Yield: Approximately 4 cups

Ingredients:

- 1 cup crudely grated or crushed jaggery, or 1¼ cups dark brown sugar
- 1 cup finely chopped mixed dried fruits, such as raisins, peaches, apricots, plums, figs, and dates
- 1 cup mango or tamarind powder, sifted to remove lumps
- 1 tablespoon peeled and finely minced fresh ginger
- 1 tablespoon vegetable oil
- 1 teaspoon black salt
- 1 teaspoon cumin seeds
- 1 teaspoon ground paprika
- 1 to 2 cups chopped ripe fruits, such as bananas, mangoes, pineapple, and peaches
- 1½ cups water + 4 cups water, measured separately
- 2 tablespoons Chaat Masala, or to taste (Homemade or store-bought)
- 2 tablespoons cumin seeds, dry-roasted and ground (See the dry-roasting section in Introduction)
- 2 teaspoons ground ginger
- 2 teaspoons salt, or to taste

Directions:

1. Immerse the dried fruits overnight in 1½ cups of the water. In the meantime, ready the cumin seeds and chaat masala. When ready, drain the fruits, reserving the water.

2. In a large non-reactive saucepan, combine the jaggery and 2 cups of the water (disregard any lumps; they will melt when heated), and bring to a boil using high heat, stirring intermittently, until all the lumps dissolve completely, about three to four minutes. Pass through a fine-mesh strainer to filter out any impurities. Return to the pan. Stir in the mango or tamarind powder and up to 2 cups water, including the reserved fruit-water in this measurement. Mix thoroughly and bring to a boil using high heat.
3. Put in the drained dried fruits, fresh and dried ginger, chaat masala, salt, and black salt, reduce the heat to moderate to low, and simmer, stirring intermittently and pouring in additional water if the sauce becomes thick too swiftly, until it reaches a semi-thick batter-like consistency, approximately ten minutes. Tweak the seasonings to your taste and move to a serving container.
4. Heat the oil in a big non-stick wok or saucepan using moderate to high heat and Put in the cumin seeds; they should sizzle upon contact with the hot oil. Swiftly, take the pan off the heat, put in the paprika, and Combine with the chutney. Serve at room temperature, or move to an airtight vessel and place in your fridge for approximately sixty days, or freeze for approximately a year. Just before serving, stir in ripe fruits and serve.

SWEET SONTH CHUTNEY WITH DATES Ⓥ

This recipe is called "Khajjur ki sonth" in Hindi

Yield: Approximately 4 cups

Ingredients:

- ½ cup seedless tamarind pulp
- ½ to ¾ cup sugar
- 1 teaspoon salt, or to taste
- 1½ tablespoons cumin seeds, dry-roasted and crudely ground (See the dry-roasting section in Introduction)
- 2 cups chopped pitted dates
- 2 cups hot water

Directions:

1. Ready the cumin seeds. Immerse the dates and tamarind pulp in 1 cup hot water, approximately one hour to soften.
2. Using your sanitized fingers, mush the pulp to separate it from the fibrous parts of the dates and to separate any tamarind seeds that may still be present. Next, pass the softened date-tamarind pulp through a fine-mesh strainer or a food mill into a big container to extract a smooth paste. Pour the rest of the hot water over the fibrous residue in the food mill and collect the rest of the pulp and Combine with the already extracted paste.
3. Move to a small saucepan, put in the sugar, cumin, and salt, and bring to a boil using high heat. Reduce the heat to moderate to low and simmer approximately five minutes. Stir in up to 1 cup of water if the chutney becomes thick too swiftly. Adjust the seasoning, then allow to cool down. Serve at room temperature, or move to an airtight vessel and place in your fridge for approximately sixty days, or freeze about a year.

ENDNOTE

Thank you for the valuable time you spend on my book. I hope it helped you at least a little, making you a slightly better Indian cook, at least. Every little bit counts! If you liked this book, don't forget to check out other books on Indian Cooking by Rekha Sharma!